Communications in Computer and Information Science   981

Commenced Publication in 2007
Founding and Former Series Editors:
Phoebe Chen, Alfredo Cuzzocrea, Xiaoyong Du, Orhun Kara, Ting Liu,
Krishna M. Sivalingam, Dominik Ślęzak, and Xiaokang Yang

Editorial Board

More information about this series at http://www.springer.com/series/7899

Graziela Simone Tonin · Bernardo Estácio
Alfredo Goldman · Eduardo Guerra (Eds.)

Agile Methods

9th Brazilian Workshop, WBMA 2018
Campinas, Brazil, October 4, 2018
Revised Selected Papers

 Springer

Editors
Graziela Simone Tonin
Federal University of Fronteira Sul
Chapecó, Santa Catarina, Brazil

Alfredo Goldman
University of Sao Paulo
Sao Paulo, São Paulo, Brazil

Bernardo Estácio
Farfetch
Porto, Portugal

Eduardo Guerra
National Institute for Space Research
São José dos Campos, São Paulo, Brazil

ISSN 1865-0929   ISSN 1865-0937 (electronic)
Communications in Computer and Information Science
ISBN 978-3-030-14309-1   ISBN 978-3-030-14310-7 (eBook)
https://doi.org/10.1007/978-3-030-14310-7

Library of Congress Control Number: 2019932787

This Springer imprint is published by the registered company Springer Nature Switzerland AG
The registered company address is: Gewerbestrasse 11, 6330 Cham, Switzerland

Preface

The 9th Brazilian Workshop on Agile Methods (WBMA 2018) was held on October 4, 2018, in Campinas, São Paulo, Brazil. The workshop is the research track in the Agile Brazil Conference. WBMA is an academic event that focuses on agile software development. This year's edition continued the history of success. Our past editions received a significant number of paper submissions with a number of attendees (students, researchers, and practitioners) from different countries. We repeated the success this year and influenced, even more, the academic integration in an industry context. We believe this integration creates ideas, opportunities, and innovations for all involved. We received 18 submissions. All the accepted papers were peer-reviewed by three referees and evaluated on the basis of technical quality, relevance, significance, and clarity. The Organizing Committee decided to accept six full papers and one short paper (40% acceptance rate). Accepted papers in this edition present empirical results and literature reviews on agile requirements validation in Brazilian software development companies, a survey on Brazilian software processes about whether to be agile or not, an evaluation of an agile maturity model, strategies to increase customer value in agile software development, a discussion toward an agile development environment, and a report on Scrum in a strongly hierarchical organization. The Organizing Committee awarded one prize in this edition, the best paper award. This CCIS volume comprises peer-reviewed versions of six full papers and one short paper. The organizers thank the Program Committee members for their contributions, and would especially like to thank all those who submitted papers, even though only a fraction could be accepted. We also thank Springer for producing these high-quality proceedings of WBMA 2018.

November 2018

Bernardo Estácio
Graziela Simone Tonin

Organization

WBMA 2018 was organized by the Agile Alliance, supported by FAPESP - process number 2018/13056-8 (Foundation for Research Support of the State of São Paulo) and Agile Brazil in cooperation with Springer.

Executive Committee

Conference Chairs

Graziela Simone Tonin   Federal University of Fronteira Sul, Brazil
Bernardo Estácio   Farfetch, Portugal

Local Chairs

Alfredo Goldman   University of São Paulo, Brazil
Eduardo Guerra   National Institute for Space Research, Brazil

Program Committee

Conference Chairs

Graziela Simone Tonin   Federal University of Fronteira Sul, Brazil
Bernardo Estácio   Farfetch, Portugal

Local Chairs

Alfredo Goldman   University of São Paulo, Brazil
Eduardo Guerra   National Institute for Space Research, Brazil

Program Committee

Adolfo Neto	Technological University of Paraná, Brazil
Alexandre Vasconcelos	Federal University of Pernambuco, Brazil
Anh Nguyen Duc	University College of Southeast, Norway
Carolyn Seaman	University of Maryland Baltimore County, USA
Célio Santana	Federal University of Pernambuco, Brazil
Fábio Levy Siqueira	University of São Paulo, Brazil
Gustavo Pinto	Federal University of Paraiba, Brazil
Hermano Moura	Federal University of Pernambuco, Brazil
Hugo Sereno Ferreira	University of Porto, Portugal
Jutta Eckstein	jeckstein.com, Germany
Liliane Fonseca	Federal University of Pernambuco, Brazil
Graziela Simone Tonin	Federal University of Fronteira Sul, Brazil

Rafael Prikladnicki	Pontifical Catholic University of Rio Grande do Sul, Brazil
Rafaela M. Fontana	Federal University of Paraná, Brazil
Raquel Aparecida Pegoraro	Federal University of Fronteira Sul, Brazil
Rodrigo Santos	Federal University of the State of Rio de Janeiro, Brazil
Tiago Silva Da Silva	Pontifical Catholic University of Rio Grande do Sul, Brazil
Viviane Santos	Federal University of Paraíba, Brazil
Wylliams Santos	University of Pernambuco, Brazil
Xiaofeng Wang	Free University of Bozen-Bolzano, Italy

Sponsoring Institutions

FAPESP (Foundation for Research Support of the State of São Paulo) and Agile Brazil.

Keynotes

Cultivating Your Personal Design Heuristics

Rebecca Wirfs-Brock

Wirfs-Brock Associate
rebecca@wirfs-brock.com

The ouroboros is an image of a serpent shaped into a circle, clinging & to or devouring its own tail in an endless cycle of self-destruction, self-creation, and self-renewal. Becoming a good software designer sometimes feels like that. How can we get better? By becoming more aware of our design heuristics and continuing to cultivate and refine them. Heuristics aid in design, guide our use of other heuristics, and even determine our attitude and behavior. For example, as agile software designers we value frequent feedback and decomposing larger design problems into smaller, more manageable chunks that we design and test as we go. We each have our own set of heuristics that we have acquired through reading, practice, and experience. This talk introduces simple ways to record design heuristics and how to share them with others. You can grow as a designer by examining and reflecting on the decisions you make and their impacts, becoming more aware of seemingly minor decisions that were more important than you thought, and putting your own spin on the advice of experts. While we may read others' design advice—be it patterns or stack overflow replies, the heuristics we've personally discovered on our own design journey may be even more important.

Sustainable Development with Agile: "Keeping Your Architecture Clean"

Joseph W. Yoder

The Refactory Inc.
joe@joeyoder.com

Being Agile, with its attention to extensive testing, frequent integration, and focusing on important product features, has proven invaluable to many software teams. When building complex systems, it can be all too easy to primarily focus on features and overlook software qualities, specifically those related to the architecture and dealing with technical debt. Some believe that by simply following Agile practices—starting as fast as possible, keeping code clean, and having lots of tests—a good clean architecture will magically emerge. While an architecture will emerge, if there is not enough attention paid to it and the code, technical debt and design problems will creep in until it becomes muddy, making it hard to deliver new features quickly and reliably. It is essential to have a sustainable architecture that can evolve through the project lifecycle. Sustainable architecture requires ongoing attention, especially when there are evolving priorities, a lot of technical risk, and many dependencies. This session will discuss elements of sustainable development specifically for dealing with technical debt. The discussion will include: choices of which problems need to be solved (upstream, how to define stories, priorities, etc); - how this development is done (downstream); - how to observe the necessary bugs and improvements in the team's backlog.

Contents

Full Papers

Agile Requirements Validation in Brazilian Software Development
Companies: A Survey 3
   Rodrigo Cursino, João Farias, Maria Lancastre, and Wylliams Santos

Are We Agile or Not? A Survey on Brazilian Software Processes 19
   *Luiz Otávio Aléssio Cesa, Rafaela Mantovani Fontana, Sheila Reinehr,
   and Andreia Malucelli*

A Tool to Measure TDD Compliance: A Case Study with Professionals 34
   Altieres de Matos, Reginaldo Ré, and Marco Aurélio Graciotto Silva

Evaluation of an Agile Maturity Model: Empirical Evidences
for Agility Assessments 49
   Adriana Corrêa Rodrigues and Rafaela Mantovani Fontana

Strategies to Increase Customer Value in Agile Software Development 63
   Fernando Sambinelli and Marcos A. F. Borges

Towards an Agile Development Environment 80
   Marcelo Lessa Ribeiro and Itana Maria de Souza Gimenes

Short Paper

Scrum in a Strongly Hierarchical Organization 97
   *Fernando Rodrigues de Sá, Everton Luiz de Resende Lucas,
   and Adelmo Dias de Oliveira*

Author Index 103

Full Papers

Agile Requirements Validation in Brazilian Software Development Companies: A Survey

Rodrigo Cursino[1,2](✉), João Farias[2](✉), Maria Lancastre[1](✉), and Wylliams Santos[1](✉)

[1] University of Pernambuco, Recife, Pernambuco, Brazil
{rbc,mlpm}@ecomp.poli.br, wbs@upe.br
[2] CESAR, Recife, Pernambuco, Brazil
jgfarias42@gmail.com

Abstract. Background: In Agile Software Development context, Requirements Engineering (RE) is an important process that happens continuously during the iterations of a product. To be able to deliver value, the teams should perform requirements validation to assure that they meet user's expectations, and also foster the collaboration between stakeholders and developers. Despite this understanding, there are still few studies that provide empirical data that make it possible to generalize the aspects, practices, and difficulties found by the teams that perform validation of agile requirements. **Goal**: The goal of this work is to understand how the requirements validation activities are being put in practice by companies of the Brazilian software industry that adopt agile methodologies. **Method**: We carried out an online survey, involving 117 participants. Our instrument focused on identifying the most used requirements artefacts, and what are the main difficulties in adopting these practices. **Results**: The results of our study reported that (i) user stories and prototypes are the most used artefacts, (ii) teams usually validate requirements by running systematic refinement meetings, and (iii) the development team and Product Owner are the most popular roles that attend to these sessions. **Conclusion**: The analysis reveals that agile teams are running requirements validation sessions as part of their development processes but they still face general RE problems, like the lack of stakeholders engagement or stakeholders that have different business visions of the same product. These results also contribute with information that allows future studies focused on the improvement of agile requirements validation.

Keywords: Requirements engineering · Requirements validation · Agile software development · Survey research

1 Introduction

When the Manifesto for Agile Software Development (ASD) was created, the authors looked for new ways to develop software, considering a new context

© Springer Nature Switzerland AG 2019
G. S. Tonin et al. (Eds.): WBMA 2018, CCIS 981, pp. 3–18, 2019.
https://doi.org/10.1007/978-3-030-14310-7_1

where the use of systems was increasingly growing and the requirements were more complex [1,6].

ASD methodologies focus on valuing people's work, understanding how to increase and improving the collaboration of the customers, stakeholders and development teams; and on delivering software with quality and value [1,19]. Other key aspect is the ability to quickly adapt to changes in requirements [10].

In this context, in order to succeed in adopting these practices, it is fundamental that teams carry out the activities and techniques of Requirements Engineering (RE). According to Pohl [15], RE is the most important phase of Software Engineering and it aims to define requirements that meet the expectations of stakeholders, considering constraints and different points of view. To make the definition of software requirements effective, it comprises several subprocesses, including elicitation, prioritization, and validation.

In ASD, these subprocesses happen continuously throughout the product development rather than in an initial phase [17,18]. The idea is that they are done in small cycles with the aim of maturing the requirements that will be implemented by the development team [12,16].

The requirements validation subprocess have a great importance in the ASD because it aims to ensure that the documented requirements are in accordance with the desires and needs of the stakeholders, as well as contribute to the early detection of errors related to the ambiguity and incompleteness of the requirements [15]. Validation activities also create opportunities for collaboration among stakeholders.

Despite understanding the importance of this subprocess, there are still few studies that provide empirical data that make it possible to generalize the aspects, practices, and difficulties found by the teams that perform validation of agile requirements [8,17]. Besides that, Wagner et al. state that the general knowledge on the current state of practice in RE is limited [21].

Consequently, the purpose of this work is to understand how the requirements validation activities are being put in practice by teams that adopt agile methodologies by carrying out an online survey with companies of the Brazilian software industry.

The reminder of this paper proceeds as follows. Section 2 presents related work. Section 3 details the methodology applied for conducting the study. Section 4 presents the results. Conclusions and future work are presented in Sect. 5.

2   Related Work

Wagner et al. [21] conducted a survey to define the state of the practice and contemporary problems in Agile RE. They build an empirical basis supported by the responses of representatives from 92 different organisation. In general, they found that "Agile RE is in several aspects not so different from RE in other development processes." Besides that, they observed that the main problems in Agile RE are about unclear requirements and communication flaws.

Furthermore, Schön et al. [18] conducted a systematic literature reviews (SLR) about Agile RE. They aimed to gather the state of the art of the literature related to RE, by looking at stakeholder and user involvement in agile methodologies. They identified 27 relevant studies and concluded that continuous communication and collaboration are the most frequent used approach to involve stakeholder in Agile RE. Besides that, they also observed that a variety of different artefacts are applied to Agile RE. The most popular ones are the user stories and prototypes.

Inayat et al. [11] also performed a SLR, focused on understanding of RE practices in agile methods. They identified 21 papers that revels 17 practices of Agile RE. Their findings also suggest that Agile RE as a research context needs additional attention and more empirical studies to better understand the impact of agile requirements engineering practices.

Ramesh et al. [17] conducted a qualitative study into Agile RE. They analysed data from 16 US software development organisations and found that intensive communication between the developers and customers is the most important RE practice.

After analysing all these related works, it is possible to observe that there is a lack of empirical studies focused on understanding the state of practice of agile requirements validation subprocess in Brazilian software development companies. Based on that, the research team decided to explore this opportunity.

3 Survey Design

Survey is a method of research aiming to gather data from a large population of interest. Despite being extensively used in software engineering, survey-based research faces several challenges [14]. In this sense, this research is supported on the guideline for conducting surveys in software engineering proposed by Linåker et al. [13].

The goal of this online survey is to better understand how the requirements validation activities are being put in practice by teams that adopt agile methodologies. It focus in companies that are from the Brazilian software industry.

3.1 Research Questions

To fulfil this overall objective, we formulated the research questions, as follows:

- RQ01. What are the techniques and practices used by them teams to perform agile requirements validation?
- RQ02. Who are the stakeholders involved in the requirements validation activities?
- RQ03. Which are the problems faced by the teams when performing requirements validation activities?
- RQ04. What are the most popular artefacts applied to Agile RE?

3.2 Target Audience

Since this study is related to requirements validation in the context of agile software development, the target audience considers professionals from companies that apply agile methodologies as part of their development processes. Also, these practitioners are members of the development team, business team or play a management role. The roles that the audience can play in their teams are listed in Table 1. In addition, the target audience is part of companies or organisations that are in the Brazilian software industry.

Table 1. Teams and roles considered as target audience.

Team	Roles
Development	- Developer
	- Tester/QA
	- Designer
	- Scrum Master
	- DevOps
Business	- Business Analyst
	- Product Owner
Management	- Project Manager
	- Agile Coach
	- Team Leader

3.3 Survey Instrument

A web-based questionnaire with a total of 23 questions was implemented to collect data. These questions were divided in the following groups: (i) demographics, (ii) agile RE artefacts, (iii) techniques and practices of requirements validation and (iv) problems faced when validating requirements. Table 2 summarises the designed questions.

The first group aims at capturing data about the respondents and their companies/organisations. With this data we are able to understand, for example, the experience with agile development and the roles played by the participants. Also, the size of the company and its maturity on the adoption of agile methodologies.

The questions of group two were designed to collect data about the artefacts used by the agile teams to document the requirements; and which of these artefacts are focus of validation.

The third one gathers data about the techniques and practices used to validate the requirements. Besides that, they aim at understanding when the validation sessions happens; and how the incidents found during these sessions are reported. Also, they focus at finding out the stakeholders who usually participate of requirements validation sessions.

Finally, the last group of questions focus on collecting data about the problems faced on running requirements validation sessions and the most common errors found during this activity.

Table 2. A summary view of the questionnaire.

Group	Id	Question	Type
Demographics	Q01	What is your name?	Open
	Q02	What is your email address?	Open
	Q03	What are the roles do you play in your current job?	Closed (MC)
	Q04	How long have you be working with agile methodologies?	Closed (SC)
	Q05	What is the size of your company?	Closed (SC)
	Q06	How do you see the adoption of agile methodologies in your company?	Closed (SC)
	...	...	...
	Q10	In which Brazilian state is your company located?	Closed (SC)
Agile RE artefacts	Q11	What are the requirements artefacts used by your team?	Closed (MC)
	Q12	What are the requirements artefacts that are focus of validation?	Closed (MC)
Requirements validation practices	Q13	What are the requirements validation techniques used in your project?	Closed (MC)
	Q14	When does the requirements validation sessions take place?	Closed (MC)
	...	...	...
	Q17	Who are the stakeholders who usually participate of requirements validation sessions?	Closed (MC)
	Q18	How important is the participation of the following stakeholders in the requirements validation process?	Likert
	...	...	...
	Q20	Could you briefly describe how the activities or requirements validation sessions are performed in your project?	Open
	...	...	...
Problems on requirements validation	Q22	Choose at least 4 types of errors found in the validation of requirements and classify them according to their criticality	Likert
	Q23	Select 4 reasons that most commonly lead to problems in requirements validation activities	Closed (MC)

The questionnaire contains a mix of open-ended and closed-ended questions. For the closed ones, the answers can be mutually exclusive single choice answers (SC) or multiple choice answers (MC). We also turn available for most of the closed MC questions the *other* option. This way, the respondents can enter their specific answers. In Q18 we used the Likert Level of Importance scale [20]: 1 - Not at all important; 2 - Low importance; 3 - Very important; 4 - Extremely important. We also added the option 5, so that the respondents can select it if the role is not present in their projects. Regarding the open questions, the respondents answer them in their own words without any required standard.

Q01 and Q02 aim to gather the participants name and email. These questions are optional and the captured data was used only when researchers needed to clarify any of the answers. For the analysis of the questions Q11 and Q12, we present a list of RE artefacts practitioners are meant to typically use in practice. This list emerged from the results of important SLRs with regards on RE practices in agile methods [11,18]. The same approach was used to question Q23. The options were selected from the results of SLRs [11,18] and other studies [12,22].

At the survey's landing page, we describe in details the goals of this research. Also, the estimated time to have the survey complete was communicated; as well as the researchers email to be used in case of any questions. Also, the survey was paginated, so that the respondents can answer few questions per page and have the sense of progress.

Pretest. Before running the survey, we carried out a pilot study using the questionnaire with a small number of participants from the target audience. This allowed us to identify some adjustments in the writing of some questions, rewrite some answers that were not so clear to understand and also balance the number of questions per page. Also, it was possible to measure the average time spent to respond the survey, which was 11 min.

3.4   Data Collection

This study used the accidental sampling design [13]. This means that the criterion for selecting the samples is the convenience. In this case, the researchers recruited subjects from their professional connections.

Each researcher prepared an invitation list including contacts from different companies and projects that use agile methodologies. Another criteria used to make these lists was to select people from different regions, so that we can have representatives from all around Brazil. Also, the survey was shared with agile methodologies user groups by using their email lists and social networks.

The data collection phase was from 2017-11-08 to 2018-04-11. Also, Survey-Monkey[1] was the tool used to build the survey and collect the data.

4   Results

In the following subsections we summarise the results of the online survey, based on the research questions. In addition, we present in Subsect. 4.1 the results related to the study population, characterising the respondents and their organisations.

---

[1] https://www.surveymonkey.com/mp/aboutus/.

4.1   Demographic Data

In total, 117 participants have completed the survey. They are from organisations from all the 5 regions of Brazil. We can find in Fig. 1(a) that most of the respondents are from companies located at the northeast (46,79%). With 25,69%, the southeast is the second region with more participants. Together, the other 3 regions were responsible for 27,52% of the collected data.

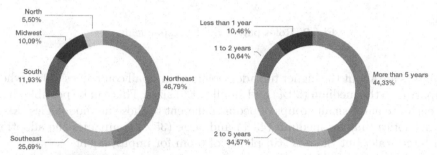

(a) Respondents per Brazilian re-   (b) Experience with agile methodologies
gions

Fig. 1. Distribution of respondents per Brazilian regions and their experience with agile methodologies.

In Fig. 1(b) we can observe that 44.33% of the respondents have more than 5 years of experience with agile methodologies. Also, 34.56% have from 2 to 5 years. Based on that, it is possible to characterise that this survey have experienced respondents. Only 20.35% of the participants have until 2 years of practices in agile.

In question Q03, the participants were asked to select all the roles they play in their projects. Figure 2 illustrates that Developer, Project Manager (PM), Scrum Master and Tester were the most selected roles. It is expected given that those (except PM) are the main roles of Scrum methodology [19]. Besides these roles, there was a good number of answers related to Business Analyst and Requirements Analyst. This is an important result since these roles are central in the requirements validation process. They usually are the authors of the requirements.

Regarding the size of the organisations, we classified them as small, medium and large. For this grouping we used the number of employees. Companies with up to 49 employees were considered small, with 50 to 99 were considered medium and with more than 100 were considered large. Based on Fig. 3(a) we can observe that 67.89% of them are large companies, 25.69% are small and only 6.42% are medium organisations.

In Fig. 3(b) we can observe the respondents perception regarding the agile methodologies adoption by their companies (per company size). We can see that there is an agile adoption-level balance regardless of company size. The

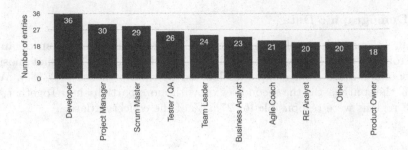

Fig. 2. Roles played by the respondents.

highlights are about the higher full adoption level in small companies (39%) when comparing to the medium (29%) and small (24%) sizes. This can be possible since it is easier to make small groups of people adherent to those methodologies. Also, we can notice that for medium (43%) and large (35%) companies the adoption is in large scale, but there is still plenty of room for improvement.

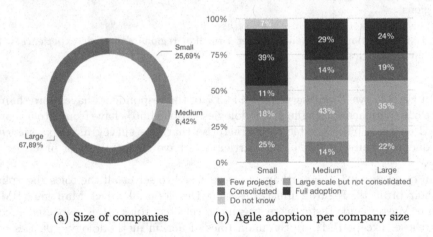

(a) Size of companies   (b) Agile adoption per company size

Fig. 3. Size of the companies and their level of agile adoption.

Figure 4(a) illustrates the distribution of the companies by sector. The majority of the respondents are from private companies (70.64%). The other 29.36% are from public organisations, most of them from universities and government companies. Those institutions can be classified in different types. Based on Fig. 4(b), we can observe that the majority of them are based on projects (38.53%) or product (33.94%). Companies are also software houses (11.01%) or base their operation in consulting (5.50%). The other data (11.01%) is about mainly to participants that works on educational institutes.

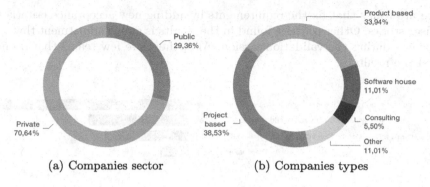

(a) Companies sector   (b) Companies types

Fig. 4. Distribution of companies per sector and their types.

4.2 RQ01 - Techniques and Practices of Agile Requirement Validation

The respondents were asked to select the practices and techniques they use to operate the agile requirements validation. Based on Fig. 5, we can observe that the majority runs requirements refinement sessions in a systematic way. Also, an important highlight is that informal reviews are still a common practice used to validate requirements. In these cases, the authors run the reviews with one or many stakeholders.

The practitioners also carry out requirements workshop at the beginning of their projects; and the teams create check-lists considering quality criteria to use them to validate agile requirements. The less selected options were related to the use of INVEST [22] best practices to support the user story writing and validation.

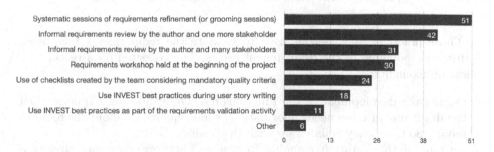

Fig. 5. Practices and techniques for agile requirements validation.

Bugs or improvements are some of the possible results of a requirements validation session. According to Fig. 6, the teams deal with these change request in a sort of different ways. They usually recorded the results as part of the meeting notes. So that, the author can work later to adjust the requirements.

There are teams that fix the requirements by adding new acceptance criteria to the user stories. Other practice found in the results is about adjustment that are performed during the validation session. Also, there are few teams that do not record the results.

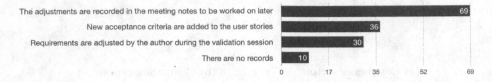

Fig. 6. The ways the teams record the requirements validation session results.

After the adjustments are done, the teams need to follow-up the updated requirements. Figure 7 reveals that most of the teams use the iteration planning meeting to look into the new versions of the documents. If the changes are minor, there is no need to set up a session to review them. Another practice is review the changes at the beginning of a recurrent refinement session. Also, depending on the impact of the updates, the team can set a new validation session. Also, there are teams that do not perform follow-up sessions.

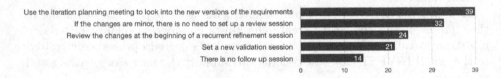

Fig. 7. How to the teams follow-up the updated requirements.

Those practices and sessions used to validate the requirements take place in different moments of the development cycles. The collected data reveals the following moments:

- During the development of the functionality. The validation happens when the development team needs information or have questions about the requirements. So that, they collaborate with the business team;
- As part of the iteration planning meetings. These meetings are already a ceremony present on the agile methodologies. The team and the stakeholders interacts to have the requirements refined and ready to be developed;
- During the current development iteration, however with a focus on refining requirements from the product backlog. This allow the authors to validate the requirements, look for improvements and understand any technical limitation in advance. This way, the requirements are stabilise before the planning meetings.

4.3   RQ02 - Stakeholders Involved in Agile Requirement Validation

This study also captured data about which are the stakeholders involved in those requirements validation sessions. We can observe on Fig. 8 that developers and Product Owners are the top 2 voted. Also, client, business analyst, Scrum Master and testers had more than 30 votes each. These are the stakeholders that perform requirements validation. In case the clients are not available, the Product Owner or business analyst are responsible to share their vision and priorities.

These results make sense and fit with other studies [2,9,18] that say the ASD projects usually are formed by two teams: development (developers, testers and Scrum Masters) and business (business analysts, client and Product Owner). They also state that the collaboration between these teams are fundamental to make sure all the different visions of the product are considered [3,5] and the requirements can be refined in a way to get them mature enough to be part of a development iteration.

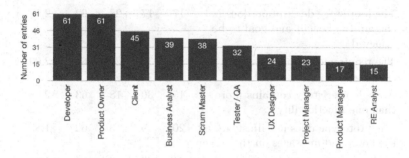

Fig. 8. Stakeholders involved in agile requirements validation.

4.4   RQ03 - Problems Faced When Performing Requirements Validation Activities

Question Q22 inquired the respondents to inform which are the common types of errors found during validation sessions of agile requirements and to classify them by criticality (the available options were Low, Medium, and High). Table 3 displays the types of error in descending order of criticality (the weighted average (WA) was calculated by assigning the value 1 to Low, 2 to Medium and value 3 to High).

Based on the set of pre-defined most common problems on agile requirements validation listed in Subsect. 3.3, the respondents were asked to rank the 4 most critical ones they face in practice. Figure 9 display the compiled ranking.

The top 2 items are related to stakeholders. The first is about the lack of client or their representatives availability. This result is also a problem present in other studies that aims to understand common problems in RE [7,8]. The second one refers to stakeholders with different views of the product. It can lead to discussions that should have been conducted prior to requirements validation.

Table 3. Most critical errors found during requirements validation sessions.

Errors	Low	Med	High	Total	WA
The requirement gives scope for multiple interpretations	6	17	47	70	2.59
The requirement is very large, making it more complex	6	21	42	69	2.52
The user story and complementary artefacts (prototype, for example) differ on the requirement	7	19	37	63	2.48
The requirement is conflicting with another already existing	5	28	32	65	2.42
The requirements do not describe all flows	10	16	34	60	2.4
The prototype does not easily illustrate the desired interaction	6	31	25	62	2.31
The user story description does not contain the benefit and goal to be achieved	17	17	28	62	2.18
The requirement is not easy to estimate	14	30	20	64	2.09
A single user story contains more than one functionality	15	30	18	63	2.05
The prototype does not illustrate all the flows and messages on the screen	20	29	13	62	1.89
Spelling mistakes	41	20	3	64	1.41

Also, a common problem selected by the respondents is regarding the moment the validation session takes place. It usually happens when the requirements are already part of a development iteration. Consequently, this context can lead to rework. Fernández et al. [7] also list it as a general problem in RE.

There are other problems that had basically the same amount of votes: the lack of qualification to run requirements validation sessions; the results of these sessions are not easily available to the team; the requirements still have primary errors that could be fixed prior to the validation meetings; or the sessions' results are not used to enhance the requirements.

The less voted problems were: the validation activity is not part of the development process, so that no time is allocated for it; and the teams consider requirements validation a repetitive and tedious activity. Based on these two results, we can infer that the agile teams are engaged on validation sessions and that this activity is present in their set of practices.

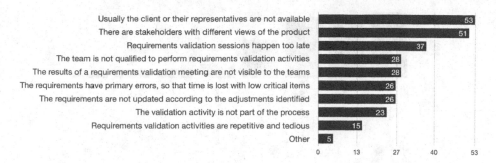

Fig. 9. Most common problems faced on agile requirements validation.

4.5 RQ04 - Most Popular Artefacts of Agile RE

In Fig. 10 we can see the word cloud with all the agile RE artefacts and the number of times they were cited by the respondents. User stories, prototypes and acceptance criteria are the most popular ones. This result is in accordance with other studies that also list these artefacts as the most used in ASD [17,18].

Acceptance test is also one of the most cited. Ramesh et al. [17] state that some organisations treat these tests as part of the requirements specification and also use them as another means for software validation. Besides that, mind map and personas had some votes.

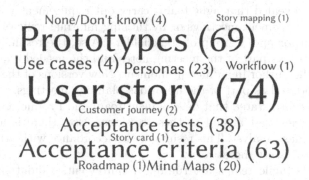

Fig. 10. Most popular artefacts used in agile RE.

Despite all these agile RE artefacts are used by the teams, only part of them are focus of validation. Figure 11 reveals that prototypes, user stories and acceptance criteria are the most present on the sessions.

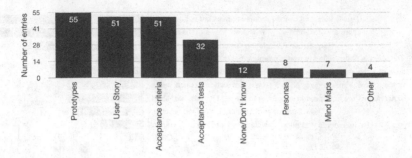

Fig. 11. Requirements artefacts target of validation.

5 Conclusions

In this article, we contributed to enhance the understanding about how Brazilian practitioners carry out requirements validation activities in their agile projects. Our analysis uses data provided by 117 participants from organisations from all the five regions of Brazil. The investigation was conducted to identify the practices used by them teams when performing agile requirements validation: (i) understand who are the stakeholders that usually attend to these sessions; (ii) analyse the problems faced by the teams when performing requirements validation; and (iii) list what are the most popular artefacts applied to Agile RE.

The survey revealed that agile teams carry out requirement validation during systematic refinement meetings or by running informal reviews between the requirement author and a group of stakeholders. Also, the results of these sessions are reported as part of the meeting notes and the needed adjustments are performed by the author in a different moment. New versions of the requirement are usually validated as part of the iterations planning meetings.

The analysis also stated that development team and Product Owner are the most popular roles that attend to these sessions. Also, there is a presence of clients and business analyst. This results are in accordance with other empirical studies that also assert theses roles.

Although the agile teams are running requirements validation sessions as part of their development processes, this survey revealed that they still face general RE problems, like the lack of stakeholders engagement or changes in requirements due to late discussions about different points of view of stakeholders [4,7,8]. Another important problem is about the moment the validation sessions happens. If it is carried out too late on the process, the requirements will not be stable enough to be developed and can lead to rework and wast problems. These results reinforce the importance of stakeholders and customer collaboration.

This survey's results also confirm what other studies [17,18] already stated: user stories, prototypes and acceptance criteria are the most popular requirements artefacts used on agile development context.

Although our study has contribute to a better understanding on agile requirement validation, we are aware that it has limitations. Our results are based on a reasonable but still limited number of respondents. Also, they are not equally distributed in all Brazilian regions. They are condensed mainly in companies from the northeast and southeast. Also, the majority of respondents are from private companies (70.64%). We can not say reliably how the picture would be if we have more representatives from public organisations. In addition, we cannot state how generalisable the results are, since we still are not able to estimate the representativeness of our population.

As future work, we believe this survey can be replicated to reach a broad and representative population; so that it can support the generalisation of the results. It should consider balance the number of participants from all the regions of Brazil. Also, invite more people from public organisations to contribute with the survey. Finally, future studies can be conducted with focus on analysing further why the problems faced when validating agile requirements happens and understand ways to mitigate them.

References

1. Beck, K., et al.: Manifesto for agile software development (2001)
2. Cao, L., Ramesh, B.: Agile requirements engineering practices: an empirical study. IEEE softw. **25**(1) (2008)
3. Cohn, M.: User Stories Applied: For Agile Software Development. Addison-Wesley Professional, Boston (2004)
4. Cursino, R., Ferreira, D., Lencastre, M., Fagundes, R., Pimentel, J.: Gamification in requirements engineering: a systematic review. In: 11th International Conference on the Quality of Information and Communications Technology (QUATIC). IEEE (2018)
5. da Silva, K.M.B., dos Santos, S.C.: Critical factors in agile software projects according to people, process and technology perspective. In: 2015 6th Brazilian Workshop on Agile Methods (WBMA), pp. 48–54. IEEE (2015)
6. Dybå, T., Dingsøyr, T.: Empirical studies of agile software development: a systematic review. Inf. Softw. Technol. **50**(9), 833–859 (2008)
7. Fernández, D.M.: Supporting requirements engineering research that industry needs: the naming the pain in requirements engineering initiative. arXiv preprint arXiv:1710.04630 (2017)
8. Fernández, D.M., et al.: Naming the pain in requirements engineering. Empirical softw. eng. **22**(5), 2298–2338 (2017)
9. Heikkilä, V.T., Damian, D., Lassenius, C., Paasivaara,M.: A mapping study on requirements engineering in agile software development. In: 2015 41st Euromicro Conference on Software Engineering and Advanced Applications (SEAA), pp. 199–207. IEEE (2015)
10. Hoda, R., Salleh, N., Grundy, J., Tee, H.M.: Systematic literature reviews in agile software development: a tertiary study. Inf. Softw. Technol. **85**, 60–70 (2017)
11. Inayat, I., Salim, S.S., Marczak, S., Daneva, M., Shamshirband, S.: A systematic literature review on agile requirements engineering practices and challenges. Comput. Hum. Behav. **51**, 915–929 (2015)

12. Leffingwell, D.: Agile Software Requirements: Lean Requirements Practices for tEams, Programs, and the Enterprise. Addison-Wesley Professional, Boston (2010)
13. Linåker, J., Sulaman, S.M., de Mello, R.M., Höst, M., Runeson, P.: Guidelines for conducting surveys in software engineering. Technical report (2015)
14. Molleri, J. S., Petersen, K., Mendes, E.: Survey guidelines in software engineering. In: Proceedings of the 10th ACM/IEEE International Symposium on Empirical Software Engineering and Measurement - ESEM 2016, pp. 1–6 (2016)
15. Pohl, K.: Requirements Engineering Fundamentals: A Study Guide for the Certified Professional for Requirements Engineering Exam-foundation Level-IREB Compliant. Rocky Nook Inc, San Rafael (2016)
16. Pressman, R.S.: Software Engineering: A Practitioner's Approach, 10th edn. McGraw-Hill Education, New York (2016)
17. Ramesh, B., Cao, L., Baskerville, R.: Agile requirements engineering practices: an empirical study. Inf. Syst. J. **20**(5), 449–480 (2010)
18. Schön, E.-M., Thomaschewski, J., Escalona, M.J.: Agile requirements engineering: a systematic literature review. Comput. Stand. Interfaces **49**, 79–91 (2017)
19. Schwaber, K., Beedle, M.: Agile Software Development with Scrum, vol. 1. Prentice Hall, Upper Saddle River (2002)
20. Vagias W.M.: Likert-type scale response anchors. Clemson (SC): Clemson International Institute for Tourism and Research Development, Department of Parks, Recreation and Tourism Management (2006)
21. Wagner, S., Fernández, D.M., Felderer, M., Kalinowski, M.: Requirements engineering practice and problems in agile projects: results from an international survey. arXiv preprint arXiv:1703.08360 (2017)
22. Wake, B.: INVEST in Good Stories: The Series (2017). (acessado em 25 de Maio de 2018)

Are We Agile or Not? A Survey on Brazilian Software Processes

Luiz Otávio Aléssio Cesa[1], Rafaela Mantovani Fontana[1(✉)], Sheila Reinehr[2], and Andreia Malucelli[2]

[1] Federal University of Paraná,
R. Dr. Alcides Vieira Arcoverde, 1225, Curitiba, PR, Brazil
{luiz.otavio,rafaela.fontana}@ufpr.br
[2] Pontifical Catholic University of Paraná,
R. Imaculada Conceição, 1155, Curitiba, PR, Brazil
sheila.reinehr@pucpr.br, malu@ppgia.pucpr.br

Abstract. How many software practitioners use agile methods in Brazil? We currently have little knowledge about Brazilian developers profile and about the software processes applied. One of the issues that remain unanswered is whether these practitioners are using agile software processes or not. With the aim to start filling this gap, we conducted a study with the objective to identify whether Brazilian software practitioners are agile. Our research approach was the survey as the method for collecting data. We applied a clustering algorithm to analyze data and characterize the software process, and text mining techniques to identify respondents perceptions of their software processes. Our results show a preliminary profile for Brazilian software processes and practitioners positive and negative perceptions about these processes. We contribute with a method to characterize agile, traditional and hybrid software processes.

Keywords: Agile software development · Practitioners survey · Software process

1 Introduction

How many software practitioners use agile methods – or "are agile" – in Brazil? Actually, we know very little about it. Softex (Association for Promoting the Excellence of Brazilian Software) performed the last government research on software and information technology (IT) services more than five years ago. They characterized the industry (number of people, revenues, among others), and mapped competencies, human resources and tendencies [25]. However, this census did not include information that is specific to software development companies, e.g., how people develop software or, more specifically, whether agile methods have spread in Brazil.

This research project is supported by CNPQ (National Council for Scientific and Technological Development) – Process Number 408976/2016-0.

G. S. Tonin et al. (Eds.): WBMA 2018, CCIS 981, pp. 19–33, 2019.
https://doi.org/10.1007/978-3-030-14310-7_2

Recent world-wide surveys have been describing developers' profiles and practices [26,27]. These researches are important because they describe current software development situation providing basis for decision makers in companies and for new studies in academy. Nevertheless, only about 2% of these results represent Brazilian situation. In academic literature, recent surveys we found with Brazilian practitioners have presented specific aspects of software development [1,14,15] but no information about software process was provided.

To start filling this gap, this study presents preliminary findings of a survey that aims at mapping whether we are agile – or not – in Brazil. The research question that drives our study is "what is the percentage of Brazilian software developers that use agile methods?". When conducting this research, we kept in mind two issues that differ from other surveys. The first was conceiving a short questionnaire that could be answered in two minutes, to increase the probability of getting bigger sample sizes [2]. The second was creating a way to identify whether practitioners' processes are agile without asking them specifically which software process models they are using. We have recent evidence that, in practice, software processes are a mix of methods [7,9], thus our research captures the essence of software process avoiding bias due to respondent's judgment.

Facing the challenges of creating a survey to be quickly answered and not asking respondent which his/her software process is, we ended up with findings not only related to the data collected, but we also provide a methodological contribution on software process mapping. Next section describes related work, Sect. 3 describes the challenge on defining a few characteristics to identify whether the software process is agile or not. Section 4 describes our research approach. Next, we present our results and, finally, discussions and conclusions.

2   Related Work

Although big companies around the world commonly perform practitioners' surveys about software development in general [26,27], recent academic surveys have been focusing on specific aspects of the practices or methods applied in software development.

The work of [10], for example, investigated software testing practices in Canada. They described the results obtained from 246 responses from local practitioners. The contributions of the authors were describing latest trends in software testing industry and pointing out strengths and weaknesses.

Other examples of industry surveys are described by [11] and [12]. The work by [11] investigated agile requirement engineering practices and their importance. Their results were based on 136 practitioners' responses mainly from US, Poland, UK, India and Germany. The study by [12] described practitioners' knowledge and perceptions of technical debt effects. They surveyed 184 practitioners from Brazil, Finland and New Zealand. These studies aimed at describing specific aspects (such as testing, requirements, technical debt) of software engineering in different countries, providing an international view of a few elements.

Differently, the work presented by [7] is a world-wide survey, but they investigated software practices in general to characterize hybrid software development.

They identified used approaches, how they are combined and how contextual factors influence the combination of different approaches for development.

Regional surveys investigating software practices in general are scarcer. We found the work by [13], which described software engineering practices in Turkey. They got 202 responses for a questionnaire with 46 questions, mainly based on Software Engineering Body of Knowledge (SWEBOK). Their findings included a general description of software development sectors, measurement methods, efforts employed in each phase of development cycle, software process models used, among others.

In Brazil, specific studies are also found, such as the one by [14], which complies a survey that described agile software development adoption, the one by [1], which presented critical success factors for software projects and the one by [15], with results from a survey about the use of Unified Modeling Language (UML) and model-driven approaches in embedded software development.

Our study contributes to the literature by presenting general findings for Brazilian software development sector and thus identifying whether practitioners use agile methods or not. Next section describes the foundation to our approach.

3 The Challenge on How to Identify an Agile Process

The simplest way to identify whether practitioners use agile methods or not is asking them: "are you agile?". The answer is not simple, though. Most software processes are not a pure application of a single method [7], once organizations customize their development processes – adopting and abandoning practices – very easily [8].

To accomplish the challenge on conducting a survey that identifies software processes, we decided thus not asking people which development methods they use. Instead, we defined our survey constructs [16] based on the literature that evaluates agile methods adoption.

The first reference to evaluate agility are the Agile Manifesto Principles [28]. According to these principles, agile software development must satisfy customers, accept requirements changes, deliver working software frequently, make developers and customers work together, build projects with motivated individuals, stimulate face-to-face conversation, measure progress with working software, promote sustainable development, stimulate technical excellence, allow team's self-organization and promote a reflective work process.

Some researchers have been working on agility assessment models, with the aim to evaluate agile adoption. These models also allow characterizing agility because they define how – in practice – agility could be identified in real teams. We analyzed four models: Sidky et al.'s [20], Qumer and Henderson Sellers' [19], Özcan-Top and Demirörs' [17,18] and Fontana's [21].

Sidky et al. [20] present the agility measurement index (SAMI). It is a five-level maturity model to determine the highest level of agility for a project or organization. For each level, more than forty agile practices are distributed through five agile principles: embrace change to deliver customer value, plan and deliver software frequently, human-centric, technical excellence and customer collaboration.

With a similar foundation as Sidky' model, Qumer and Henderson-Sellers [19] present the Agile Adoption and Improvement Model (AAIM). The model identifies six stages for agile improvement, based on agile principles. Each stage defines a group of practices to be implemented starting with an "Agile Infancy", passing through "Agile Initial", "Agile Realization", "Agile Value", "Agile Smart", and getting to an "Agile Progress".

Özcan-Top and Demirös [18] present the Software Agility Assessment Model (AgilityMOD). The content in their paper is complemented by a technical report [17]. This model was developed based on ISO/IEC 15504 International Standard. They defined aspects attributes grouped into agility levels. Each aspect attribute is related to agile principles and are defined as: "Performing Aspect Practices", in the first level; "Simple" and "Iterative", in the second level; "Technically Excellent", in the third level; and "Learning" for the fourth level. The agility of one aspect is, then, evaluated in a four-point scale: "Not implemented", "Ad-hoc", "Lean" and "Effective", which are the agility levels.

The most recent work we found was the one presented by Fontana et al. [21]. The authors proposed the Agile Compass, a tool to identify maturity in agile software development teams. This tool was developed based on an empirical study that identified the evolvement of nine agile teams. Their proposal is not based on levels, but on outcomes that teams should pursue. There is therefore no specific path to maturity. Authors identified seven categories of outcomes: practices learning, team conduct, pace of deliveries, features disclosure, software product, customer relationship and organizational support.

We have extracted from each of these authors the characteristics of agility, by analyzing how they defined a mature team, that is, a team that is actually agile, as described in Table 1. We also analyzed the agile principles defined in the Agile Manifesto [28] and chose three of them. The characteristics of Sidky et al. [20] were not included because they proposed more than 40 items do define agility and it would go against our purpose of a short questionnaire. As our proposal was to create a short survey, we selected only the characteristics that were straightforward to be evaluated and did not involve discussions about organizational culture and personnel issues.

By combining the characteristics of agility selected from these studies, we identified that they were related to four main aspects of the software process: requirements definition (based on characteristics 1, 6, and 10), software documentation (based on characteristic 3), development activities planning (based on characteristics 5 and 8) and delivery of working software (based on characteristics 2, 4, 7, and 9).

We understand that the essence in the difference between traditional and agile processes is the *moment* when each of these aspects are emphasized during software development, as *dynamism* is one of the key differences between the two approaches [23]. We then based our survey in this assumption, as explained in the next section.

Table 1. Characteristics for agility evaluation from literature.

Author	Characteristic	Selected (id)
Agile Manifesto	Accept changes in requirements	X (1)
	Foster delivery of working software frequently	X (2)
	Face-to-face communication as the effective way to convey information	X (3)
Özcan-Top and Demirörs	Develop work products in an iterative and incremental way	X (4)
	Communicate effectively	
	Balance the predictive work and adaptive work	X (5)
	Employ minimally sufficient ceremony	
	Incorporate agile engineering methods/practices to the aspect practices	
	Integrate tools to aspects to improve the productivity	
	Support collaborative work and shared responsibility	
	Adopt agile leadership styles and adjust the behaviors towards mistakes of people	
	Encourage people in the organization to participate in learning, teaching and improvement	
	Collect measures to support learning and improvement	
Qumer and Henderson-Sellers	Does the method accommodate expected or unexpected changes? (Flexibility)	X (6)
	Does the method produce results quickly? (Speed)	X (7)
	Does the method follow the shortest time span, use economical, simple and quality instruments for production? (Leanness)	
	Does the method apply updated prior knowledge and experience to create a learning environment? (Learning)	
	Does the method exhibit sensitiveness? (Responsiveness)	X (8)
Fontana et al.	The team improves its own work processes	
	Metrics are used for improvement and learning	
	The team makes decisions about the project and about the process	
	The team wished to learn and improve technically	
	The team delivers within the due date	X (9)
	The team accepts changes to requirements throughout the project	X (10)
	The team worries about the quality of the source code	
	The team uses tools to make development more effective	
	The customer trusts in team's work	
	The organization prioritizes agility as the strategy for software development	

4   Research Approach

The objective of this study was identifying the percentage of Brazilian software practitioners using agile software development methods. The research approach was the survey, defined by [16] as a method that collects information from individuals to contribute to knowledge in a particular area of interest. Our results are descriptive, as we aim at describing the distribution of a phenomenon – agile methods usage, in a population – software development practitioners [16].

According to Forza [16], conducting a survey must include the following subprocesses that lead to getting the desired results: (1) translating the theoretical domain into the empirical domain; (2) designing and pilot testing; (3) collecting data for theory testing; (4) data analysis process; and (5) the process of interpreting the results and writing the report. Next subsections describe how the first four of these subprocesses were performed in this study.

4.1   Translation of the Theoretical Domain into the Empirical Domain

As described in Sect. 3, we investigated studies that defined how to characterize and evaluate agility [18–21], besides considering the definitions of the Agile Manifesto principles [28]. Our unit of analysis was the software development practitioner, as a representative of the method used inside companies.

We avoided asking respondents which methods or approaches they use for software development, as evidences from modern software development show that processes and practices are mixed and combined [7,9]. Asking a respondent to classify its own process would lead to potentially subjective decisions when answering the questionnaire. For example, does the simple definition of sprints in a software project planning characterize the use of Scrum? An inexperienced developer could say that yes, but the reality might not be that. This is the reason we based our questionnaire in studies that characterize and evaluate agility despite of the method used.

From these theoretical and empirical references, we extracted a minimum number of items that could in a straightforward way to characterize agility and allow our respondents to quickly answer our questions. We based our definitions on the premise of creating a short questionnaire that could be answered in two minutes. As stated by Pfleeger and Kitchenham [3, p. 21], "it is important to keep in mind that the number of questions you can realistically ask in a survey depends on the amount of time respondents are willing to commit to it". We wanted to potentially increase sample size by creating a questionnaire that could be answered by more people [2].

Section 3 showed the characteristics extracted from each author and how they were combined to create the questionnaire. Respondents were asked to place these aspects in specific moments in their software processes, using as a reference the moment when software is coded. The final questionnaire was really short, comprising:

1. In which state of Brazil do you work at?
2. How many years of experience do you have with software development?
3. What is your educational level?
4. What is your gender?
5. In the software project you are currently working, please identify in which moment the following activities happen (before coding, throughout coding, after coding, or do not know):
   (a) Requirements definition
   (b) Software documentation
   (c) Development activities planning
   (d) Delivering working software
6. Summarize the <u>positive</u> aspects of your software process using 5 key-words (open-ended question)
7. Summarize the <u>negative</u> aspects of your software process using 5 key-words (open-ended question).

4.2 Design and Pilot Testing

The questionnaire was designed and pilot-tested in two steps: a focus group and a pilot study. For the focus group, the first version was created, printed and tested with 10 master and doctorate students. They evaluated language, form and response time. The suggestions were accepted and the tested version was completely changed to the final version.

This final version was created on-line and pilot-tested with 25 software practitioners in authors' colleagues network. In addition to answering the questions of the questionnaire, we asked them to tell us whether their processes were agile, traditional or hybrid. We did it to test the clustering techniques we were planning to apply for data analysis (see Sect. 4.4). The responses were processed, and data analysis was tested. The question on which process the respondent used was removed for the questionnaire to be distributed.

4.3 Collecting Data

Sampling is a concern in surveys, as samples must be representative of the whole population. Ideally, all surveys should use random samples, as they are the only format that create statistically valid results [2]. In this study it was not possible as we do not have access to the whole population (all software developers in Brazil), thus we applied a non-probabilistic convenience sample.

Convenience samples are those that represent people that are available and willing to take part of the survey [2]. We used social networks and personal contacts to propagate the call for respondents. We made our questionnaire available on-line for two weeks.

4.4   Data Analysis

We applied three different types of data analysis: clustering, descriptive statistics and text mining. The clustering technique was applied to group respondents according to similar software processes. We analyzed the moment in which the respondent defined requirements, documented software, planned activities and delivered software. Responses were grouped using the k-means algorithm through R language (libraries RWeka and cluster). We defined three resulting clusters, and, for each cluster, we used a histogram to identify how answers were distributed in the different moments (before, throughout or after coding).

We chose to create three clusters to possibly accommodate agile processes, traditional processes[1] and a third group that could show up with different characteristics (such as the hybrid processes defended by [7]).

The text mining technique was used to analyze the two open-ended questions. The answers given by respondents to the positive and negative aspects of their software processes were analyzed using a frequency of terms analysis (by using the tm library from R language). We first analyzed the frequency of terms individually and then the frequency of bi-grams. Individual terms analysis allows us to identify most cited terms and then the analysis of related bi-grams eases the understanding of the context where terms were cited in responses.

4.5   Threats to Validity

There are four types of validity to be dealt with in survey studies. The face validity guarantees that the measure reflects the content of the concept in question [22]; the content validity, which is a "subjective assessment of how appropriate the instrument seems to a group of reviewers" [4, p. 22]; the criterion validity, which compares the instrument against one that is considered the "gold standard" [4, p. 22]; and the construct validity that concerns "how an instrument behaves when used" [4, p. 22]. In this research, content and construct validity were tested in the focus group and in the pilot-test. Criterion validity could not be measured, as we do not have a "gold standard" as reference.

Generalization is also a concern in surveys. Although [22] states that increasing the absolute number of respondents in the sample does not increase generalization, it is know that the more respondents, the lower the error rate in the results. With about a hundred respondents, we consider that the results of this study represent practical relevance, which means that it matters to practitioners [5]. This study presents preliminary results, as we wish to continue collecting data to compare with the findings here presented. This is one of the strategies that can be applied to assure practical relevance in a research [6].

5   Results

We received 129 valid responses. Respondents were 81% male and 19% female. Their educational level was 2% high school, 40% undergraduate, 11% MBA

---

[1] As opposed to agile, traditional processes could also be called plan-driven processes, such as stated by [23].

(Master Business Administration), 34% attended post-graduation courses, 11% had master degree and 2% doctoral degree. Their experience with software development was 20% up to 2 years; 26% from 3 to 5 years; 28% from 6 to 10 years; 26% from 11 to 20 years and 5% more than 20 years. Considering their location in Brazil, they are distributed in ten different states, as shown in Table 2.

Table 2. Distribution of respondents in Brazil.

State	Percentage (%)
PR	48
MG	22
SP	15
SC	5
PE, DF, RS, AL, MS, PA	10

Our driving objective in this study was to discover the percentage of software developers that use agile methods in Brazil. As explained in Sect. 4, we identified it by asking about some dynamics in their software processes. The responses were then clustered in three groups according to the similarity of the answers practitioners gave regarding the moment in which they define requirements, document the software, plan activities and deliver software. As a result of the clustering algorithm, we got 54% of respondents in Group 1, 26% in Group 2 and 20% in Group 3. The characteristics of each group are as follows.

Figure 1 shows the results for Group 1. The answers in this cluster reported to define requirements mainly before coding (96% of respondents). They document software mainly throughout coding (64%), but also before coding (36%). Regarding the planning of development activities, they reported to perform mostly before coding (69%) and some throughout coding (31%). Their software delivery is mainly performed after coding (60%), but also throughout coding (38%).

The second group that resulted from the clustering analysis presents a different behavior (see Fig. 2). They reported to define requirements mainly before coding (82%), and some of them throughout coding (18%). Their software documentation is performed mainly after coding (71%). On respect to development activities planning, respondents said that it is done mainly before coding (68%) and a few throughout coding (26%). For them, software is delivered mainly after coding (76%), and some reported to do it throughout coding (21% of responses).

Group 3 (Fig. 3) presents another configuration of responses distribution. On respect to requirements definition, they reported to do it mainly throughout coding (80% of responses). Software is documented either throughout coding (52%) and after coding (40%). Activities are planned also throughout coding (56%) and before coding (40% of responses). For this group, software is delivered mainly throughout coding (84%).

According to the characteristics of these groups, by comparing the different moments when activities are performed, we observe clear evidences of the essence

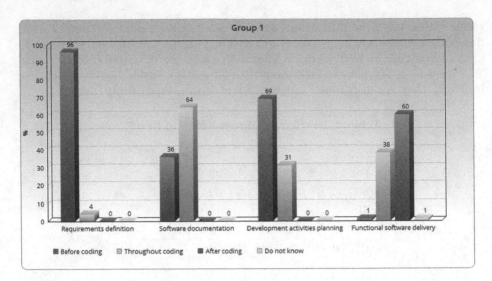

Fig. 1. The moment when practitioners perform their software process activities in Group 1.

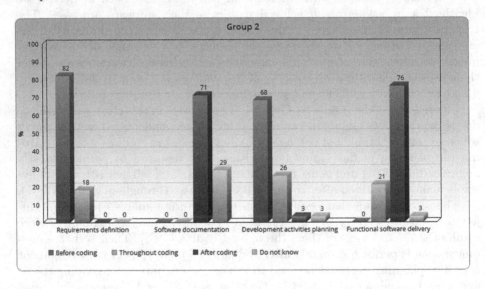

Fig. 2. The moment when practitioners perform their software process activities in Group 2.

of their software processes. Group 1 is the *hybrid group*, mainly because there is a distribution of requirements and planning before and throughout coding. Delivery is also performed throughout and after coding. Group 2 is the *traditional group*, with the evidences of requirements and planning being performed mainly before coding, and delivery mainly after coding. The *agile group* is the Group

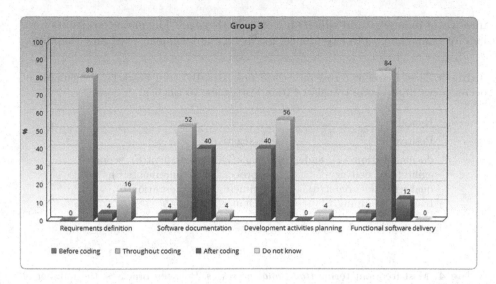

Fig. 3. The moment when practitioners perform their software process activities in Group 3.

3, with requirements definition mainly throughout coding, activities planning before and throughout coding, and software delivery mainly throughout coding.

As Group 1 was the one with more respondents, we conclude, then, that we have mainly software development practitioners working with hybrid processes in Brazil (54%), then with traditional processes (26%) and the least number of practitioners are the ones that work with agile processes (20%).

We also asked respondents about positive and negative aspects of their processes. We analyzed the responses for each of the groups separately so that we could then better characterize them, as shown in the next subsection.

5.1 Perceptions on the Software Process

Positive and negative aspects of software processes were pointed out by respondents through keywords. We considered the terms that appeared the most, the top-3 frequencies. Table 3 shows terms frequencies for hybrid processes, Table 4 shows for traditional processes and Table 5 for agile processes.

We can notice that positive aspects of *hybrid processes* are mainly related to documentation and agility/agile. In the analysis of software process activities moments (Sect. 5) this group pointed out to document software before and throughout coding, which is shown here to be positive for practitioners. By analyzing related bi-grams, we observe that practitioners value consistent and viable documentation and various aspects related to agility (projects, delivery, flexibility, quality, etc.). We also found positive key-words related to delivery, quality, customer, team and planning. The main negative aspect pointed out by the hybrid group was "lack". In this case, the analysis of the bi-grams was important to understand which kind of lacks they feel. The main complaints were lack of communication, experience, feedback, management, staff and visibility.

Table 3. Most frequent terms for *hybrid processes*. Between brackets, the number of occurrences. Terms were translated from Portuguese to English.

Hybrid	
Positive	Negative
documentation(11), agile(10), agility(10), delivery(7), quality(7), customer(6), team(6), planning(6)	lack(7), development(6), scope(6), process(6), requirements(6), time(6), documentation(5), change(5), tests(5)

Table 4. Most frequent terms *traditional processes*. Between brackets, the number of occurrences. Terms were translated from Portuguese to English.

Traditional	
Positive	Negative
agility(8), delivery(8), agile(5), customer(4), quality(4)	lack(9), low(3), documentation(3), requirements(3), tests(3)

For the *traditional processes* group, the positive aspects are mainly related to agility/agile and delivery. It seems to be contradictory that people that use traditional processes value agility. But this is probably due to the fact that people do mix processes and present some evidences of trial to be agile. By analyzing related bi-grams, we could notice that practitioners related agile and agility to collaboration, reliability, delivery, focus. Other positive aspects also mentioned were focusing at customer and quality. As negative aspects for the traditional group, we identified "lacks", but, differently of hybrid processes, the terms that appeared were lack of empathy, capacity, knowledge, control, documentation, metrics, quality assurance, resources. The "low" term was referred to quality and resilience.

For the *agile processes* group, the most frequent positive aspects were also related to agility and delivery. Related bi-grams show terms as adaptive agile, agile delivery, dynamics, fast delivery, value delivery, among others. Negative terms appeared mainly related to documentation (missing of documentation, late documentation, stress related to documentation, time to document). By combining this data with the moments when they perform they activities, we see software being documented throughout and after coding, which seems to be negative for this group. There were also complaints of "lack": of knowledge, staff, information, planning and requirements. The only group where "bugs" appeared in negative aspects was the agile one. Other terms are presented in Table 5.

Table 5. Most frequent terms for *agile processes*. Between brackets, the number of occurrences. Terms were translated from Portuguese to English.

Agile	
Positive	Negative
agility(7), delivery(5), agile(4), development(4)	documentation(7), lack(7), time(4), bugs(3), team(3), indefiniteness(3), requirements(3), rework(3), risks(3), tests(3)

6 Discussion and Conclusions

The objective of this study was to identify the percentage of software development practitioners that use agile methods in Brazil. We identified that this is the least used method, reported by 20% of participants, as opposed to traditional methods, reported by 26%, and the most used, the hybrid process, reported by 54% of respondents.

To accomplish this objective, we did not ask practitioners whether they were agile. We instead asked objective questions about activities in their software processes and inferred their characteristics based on a clustering analysis. We also searched for positive and negative aspects of different process configurations.

Our results are in accordance with evidences that software processes are highly customized [8,9]. We saw most respondents taking part of a hybrid process that presents agile and traditional characteristics. It is an evidence that we are probably living what Boehm and Turner [23] previewed more than a decade ago, a balance and integration of agile and plan-driven methods. Despite of the process model used, agility was pointed out as a positive aspect in all of them, evidencing the willing to be agile.

Some years ago, the work by [14] showed that the usage of agile methods was rising, as also stated by agile industrial surveys [29]. With our results we consider people are using agile, but not as the "silver bullet". Agile practices are mixed with traditional ones because software development practitioners actually focus on having the job done [24].

Our results are limited to our sample. As we stated, we consider these as preliminary results, as we wish to collect more responses for this survey and complete and compare data. Nevertheless, these findings show evidence of Brazilian software processes and provide basis for other academic studies that might wish to better understand the dynamics of the aspects we investigated in the software process. Our method to characterize the software process could also be replicated and retested in other configurations.

References

1. Dal Forno, G.M.B., Muller, F.M.: Fatores Críticos em Projetos de Desenvolvimento de Software. In: Pretexto 2017, vol. 18, no. 2, pp. 100–105 (2017). https://doi.org/ 10.21714/pretexto.v18i2.5295
2. Pfleeger, S.L., Kitchenham, B.A.: Principles of survey research - part 5: populations and samples. Softw. Eng. Notes **27**(5), 17–20 (2002)
3. Pfleeger, S.L., Kitchenham, B.A.: Principles of survey research - part 3: constructing a survey instrument. Softw. Eng. Notes **27**(2), 20–24 (2002)
4. Pfleeger, S.L., Kitchenham, B.A.: Principles of survey research - part 4: questionnaire evaluation. Softw. Eng. Notes **27**(3), 20–23 (2002)
5. Kitchenham, B.A., et al.: Preliminary guidelines for empirical research in software engineering. IEEE Trans. Softw. Eng. **28**, 721–734 (2002). https://doi.org/10.1109/ TSE.2002.1027796
6. Lee, A.S., Mohareji, K.: Linking relevance to practical significance. In: Proceedings of the 45th Hawaii International Conference on System Sciences, Maui, 4–7 January, pp. 5234–5240 (2012). https://doi.org/10.1109/HICSS.2012.416
7. Kuhrman, M., et al.: Hybrid software and system development in practice: waterfall, scrum and beyond. In: Proceedings of the 2017 International Conference on Software and System Process, ICSSP 2017, France, pp. 30–39 (2017). https://doi. org/10.1145/3084100.3084104
8. Bustard, D., Wilkie, G., Greer, D.: The maturation of agile software development principles and practice: observations on successive industrial studies in 2010 and 2012. In: Proceedings of the International Conference and Workshops on the Engineering of Computer Based Systems, Scottsdale, AZ, pp. 139–146. IEEE (2013)
9. Campanelli, A.S., Camilo, R.D., Parreiras, F.S.: The impact of tailoring criteria on agile practices adoption: a survey with novice agile practitioners in Brazil. J. Syst. Softw. **137**, 366–379 (2018). https://doi.org/10.1016/j.jss.2017.12.012
10. Garousi, V., Zhi, J.: A survey of software testing practices in Canada. J. Syst. Softw. **86**(5), 1354–1379 (2013). https://doi.org/10.1016/j.jss.2012.12.051
11. Ochodek, M., Zopczyńska, S.: Perceived importance of agile requirements engineering practices - a survey. J. Syst. Softw. **143**, 29–43 (2018). https://doi.org/10. 1016/j.jss.2018.05.012
12. Holvitie, J., et al.: Technical debt and agile software development practices and processes: an industry practitioner survey. Inf. Softw. Technol. **96**, 141–160 (2018). https://doi.org/10.1016/j.infsof.2017.11.015
13. Garousi, V., Coskunçay, A., Betin-Can, A., Demirörs, O.: A survey of software engineering practices in Turkey. J. Syst. Softw. **108**, 148–177 (2015). https://doi. org/10.1016/j.jss.2015.06.036
14. Melo, C., et al.: The evolution of agile software development in Brazil. J. Braz. Comput. Soc. **19**, 523–552 (2013). https://doi.org/10.1007/s13173-013-0114-x
15. Agner, L.T.W., Soares, I.W., Stadzisz, P.C., Simão, J.M.: A Brazilian survey on UML and model-driven practices for embedded software development. J. Syst. Softw. **86**(4), 997–1005 (2013). https://doi.org/10.1016/j.jss.2012.11.023
16. Forza, C.: Survey research in operations management: a process-based perspective. Int. J. Oper. Prod. Manag. **22**(2), 152–194 (2002)
17. Özcan-Top, Ö., Demirörs, O.: Software agility assessment reference model v 3.0 (Agility MOD). Technical report METU/II-TR-2014-39 (2014)

18. Özcan-Top, Ö., Demirörs, O.: Assessing software agility: an exploratory case study. In: Mitasiunas, A., Rout, T., O'Connor, R.V., Dorling, A. (eds.) SPICE 2014. CCIS, vol. 477, pp. 202–213. Springer, Cham (2014). https://doi.org/10.1007/978-3-319-13036-1_18

19. Qumer, A., Henderson-Sellers, B.: A framework to support the evaluation, adoption and improvement of agile methods in practice. J. Syst. Softw. **81**(11), 1899–1919 (2008). https://doi.org/10.1016/j.jss.2007.12.806

20. Sidky, A., Arthur, J., Bohner, S.: A disciplined approach to adopting agile practices: the agile adoption framework. Innov. Syst. Softw. Eng. **3**(3), 203–216 (2007). https://doi.org/10.1007/s11334-007-0026-z

21. Fontana, R.M., Reinehr, S., Malucelli, A.: Agile compass: a tool for identifying maturity in agile software-development teams. IEEE Softw. **32**(6), 20–23 (2015). https://doi.org/10.1109/MS.2015.135

22. Bryman, A.: Social Research Methods, 4th edn. Oxford University Press, New York (2012)

23. Boehm, B., Turner, R.: Balancing agility and discipline: evaluating and integrating agile and plan-driven methods. In: Proceedings of the 26th International Conference on Software Engineering, 23–28 May, pp. 718–719 (2004). https://doi.org/10.1109/ICSE.2004.1317503

24. Adolph, S., Krutchen, P., Hall, W.: Reconciling perspectives: a grounded theory of how people manage the process of software development. J. Syst. Softw. **85**, 1269–1286 (2012). https://doi.org/10.1016/j.jss.2012.01.059

25. Softex: Software e servićos de TI: A Indústria Brasileira em Perspectiva (2012). http://www.softex.br/inteligencia/. Accessed 9 July 2018

26. Stackoverflow: Developers survey results (2018). https://insights.stackoverflow.com/survey/2018/. Accessed 9 July 2018

27. O'Reilly: O'Reilly Software Development Salary Survey (2017). https://www.oreilly.com/ideas/2017-software-development-salary-survey. Accessed 9 July 2018

28. Agile Manifesto Principles (2001). http://agilemanifesto.org/principles.html. Accessed 9 July 2018

29. Version One: 12th State of Agile Survey (2018). http://stateofagile.versionone.com/. Accessed 12 July 2018

A Tool to Measure TDD Compliance:
A Case Study with Professionals

Altieres de Matos[1], Reginaldo Ré[2(✉)], and Marco Aurélio Graciotto Silva[1,2]

[1] Graduate Program in Informatics (PPGI),
Federal University of Technology – Paraná (UTFPR),
Cornélio Procópio, Paraná, Brazil
`altitdb@gmail.com`
[2] Department of Computing (DACOM),
Federal University of Technology – Paraná (UTFPR),
Campo Mourão, Paraná, Brazil
`{reginaldo,magsilva}@utfpr.edu.br`

Abstract. Context: There are several studies related to Test Driven Development (TDD), but many with divergences of results due to the short time to perform the experiments. Moreover, the environment where they are carried out is generally academic. On the other hand, the environment requires tools not used by practitioners or imposes many technical and training requirements for their application. **Goal:** The goal of this paper is to provide a tool that supports the evaluation of the TDD process in the software industry and academia settings. The tool focuses on analyzing the effects of verification, validation and test (VV&T). In addition, the compliance of TDD usage in software development was evaluated. **Method:** This study made use of the Goal Question Metric (GQM) paradigm to characterize a set of objectives using metrics towards TDD effects on software quality. A case study was conducted with IT professionals to evaluate the tool developed. **Results:** Considering the existing tools that perform TDD compliance assessment, the Butterfly tool was developed to enable the evaluation of the TDD lifecycle as the developer performs the coding of the software. With this tool it is possible to analyze the compliance of TDD usage during software development. **Conclusions:** The tool allows to measure the effects of TDD when developing software, which will support in the characterization of TDD contributions and interventions applied to software quality in future works.

Keywords: Test driven development · Agile software development ·
TDD conformance · TDD lifecycle · Software measurement

1 Introduction

Test Driven Development (TDD) provides developers with the ability to write small pieces of software based on software requirements, implementing test cases

© Springer Nature Switzerland AG 2019
G. S. Tonin et al. (Eds.): WBMA 2018, CCIS 981, pp. 34–48, 2019.
https://doi.org/10.1007/978-3-030-14310-7_3

before production code [9,20]. Thus, each piece of code and its respective automatic test is written in a cycle [9]. This style of development enables developers to stay focused on requirements sets, ensuring that every piece of written production code is covered by automated tests [9,20].

TDD is considered an agile practice related to quality [6,13]. With the introduction of TDD in eXtreme Programming (XP) and its frequent use in conjunction with the Scrum agile method [12], TDD has gained popularity [2,6]. However, despite its adoption in software industry, several aspects regarding TDD, such as conformance and software testing activities, are not focused by the research community [16].

The motivation of this study lies in the fact that the software industry and academia are not strongly connected and do not have high collaboration between them [5]. In the software testing domain, one of the main problems is that researchers are not worried about solving problems of the software industry [10]. Several reasons regarding this have been discussed by software engineering researchers, from the difference of objectives between the two parties to challenges of scalability and applicability of problems [10].

One of the current discussions in the area of software testing is the compulsory testing of software in the scope of software development [5,18]. Another motivating factor is the increase in the interest of professionals in test automation [18]. In contrast, there are factors that limit the adoption of TDD in the software industry: (i) increased development time, (ii) insufficient experience and knowledge about TDD, (iii) lack of upfront design, (iv) insufficient developer testing skills, (v) lack of adherence to the TDD protocol, (vi) limitations regarding TDD implementation related to domain and tools, and (vii) legacy code [7]. In addition to these factors, it is observed that, currently, the adoption of agile methods requires that the responsibility for software quality be made beyond the quality team [8]. If, in agile methods, it is argued that teams have autonomy and that they are responsible for the software, it is sensible to give them greater responsibility for software quality, rather than delegating such a role integrally to a distinct part (such as a quality assurance team).

Although global software development industry and the software research academy have a large number of members, collaboration between the two is low [10]. In 2017, the state of the art software testing considered that performing manual or automatic testing became mandatory for the production of software products [5]. In this way, adopting TDD makes it possible to go further [20]. TDD provides the industry the possibility to improve adherence to proper software testing activities, minimizing the chances of skimping on the implementation of test cases after writing production code [20].

This study aims to provide a tool to support the evaluation of the TDD process in the academia and software industry. A fundamental aspect of the study is the application in the software industry encompassed in the agile context along with the use of the iterative model. The tool allows the real-time analysis of coding performed by developers, classifying their actions regarding editing test cases and code and, considering such actions, classify the development cycle/iteration in: (i) test-addition, (ii) test-first, (iii) test-last, (iv) test driven development, (v) refactoring e (vi) unknown. Thus, conformance to TDD can be evaluated through the classifications and other measurements regarding testing activities, such as test coverage and quantity of implemented test cases.

Some studies that evaluate TDD usage in the software industry and TDD conformance are described in Sect. 2. Considering their findings and the limitations regarding tool support for TDD adoption, the tool, named Butterfly, is described in Sect. 3. Afterwards, in Sect. 4, it was provided details of the case study used to evaluate the developed tool, describing the results in Sect. 5 and discussing how the tool can influence the community in Sect. 6. Conclusions and next steps regarding the investigation on the integration of TDD and software testing within the industry setting are presented in Sect. 7.

2   Related Work

Test Driven Development (TDD) [3] is an iterative software development technique [9,19]. In the TDD process, each new iteration consists of the implementation of a feature [9]. Three phases make up the TDD process: (i) writing the unit test, (ii) implementing the production code, and (iii) refactoring [9,19]. The iteration begins with writing the unit test, followed by the implementation phase of the production code, and finalizing itself in the refactoring phase [9,19]. The iteration is terminated when all phases of the process are executed and the unit tests are successfully executed [9]. The main rule of TDD is: *"If you can't write a test for what you are about to code, then you shouldn't even be thinking about coding"* [11].

TDD and some of its effects have been extensively studied [9]. Considering the objective of this study, it was focused on related work regarding TDD conformance, helping developers with the use of TDD and improving software design, so that it was possible to obtain the best solution for the desired scenario [17].

In the study by Kou et al. [15], the authors presented a tool that allows automated recognition of TDD. The so called Zorro system allows the operational definition of TDD practices to be verified. The automated recognition of TDD can bring several benefits to the community, either to support TDD practices or to assist in empirical studies on the effectiveness of TDD. The study described how the analysis can be performed with the Zorro system, in addition to two empirical assessments. The first controlled experiment aimed to ensure that the collected and analyzed information was appropriate and effective. In the second controlled experiment conducted by the authors, they aimed to obtain better data about the strengths and limitations of Zorro for TDD inference. A third controlled experiment was conducted in order to address a validity threats. Thus, the authors did not use students as subjects, as in the two previous controlled experiments, besides not using the classroom environment. Instead, the authors run the controlled experiment with professionals of the software industry. The study fostered the possibility of tool evolution, in order to improve its ability to recognize TDD processes, in addition to providing information in a clear and objective way. It also made it possible to evaluate the effects of TDD in the medium and long term with respect to software quality.

In the study by Becker et al. [4], the authors presented the Besouro tool, which is an improved version of their previous TDD automatic recognition tools and studies. The following tools were used: (i) TestFirstGauge, (ii) TDDGuide, (iii) Zorro and (iv) SEEKE. The authors compared them with other existing tools and commented on the new features existing in the Besouro, some of them being built with private (closed-source) components. The Besouro tool shares several concepts used in the Zorro tool of the study by Kou et al. [15]. To verify the effectiveness of the tool, the authors performed a controlled experiment that was defined through the GQM model (goal, question and metrics). Given this model, the authors defined the following objective: "Analyze the variations of an operational definition of TDD to evaluate with respect to TDD compliance criteria from the perspective of the developers in the context of programming activities". The authors considered the Besouro tool as a potential system for conducting quantitative TDD studies.

In the study by Fucci et al. [9], the authors presented an extensive study on TDD processes. As a goal, the authors sought to find out the impact of the effects that the TDD process characteristics can have on the external quality of the software and the productivity of the developers. The authors identified four characteristics in the TDD process, detailed in Table 1: (i) granularity, (ii) uniformity, (iii) sequence and (iv) refactoring effort.

Table 1. Characteristics corresponding to TDD processes [9].

Characteristic	Definition
(i) Granularity	Characterized by a short development process, where each cycle typically lasts between 5 and 10 min
(ii) Uniformity	Characterized by development cycles that last approximately the same time
(iii) Sequence	Indicates the prevalence of the test-first (TF) sequence during the development process
(iv) Refactoring effort	Indicates the prevalence of refactoring activity in the development process

The authors conducted a quasi-experiment in the context of the software industry. For the production of the data, the authors performed four workshops with themes on unit tests, TDD, TF, TL and iterative process of unit tests. Each workshop lasted five days. To obtain the data of the development cycles, the authors used the tool Besouro [4]. The data generated by the tool were used to calculate metrics that represent the TDD characteristics described in Table 1. Within their study, it was possible to conclude that the benefits of TDD are not only provided by the dynamics of test first (TF). TDD as a process encourages developers to follow fine and steady steps by improving the focus and flow of development [9].

Even with a number of tools designed to recognize the TDD lifecycle processes, no completely open source tools for this purpose in the community was found. There is also the need for effective analysis and summarization of data generated by the tools. Building an open-source tool free of private components is a differential against existing tools in the community, providing an increase in the maintainability and easing the evolution of the tool.

3 Butterfly Tool

To develop the **Butterfly** tool it was necessary to evolve heuristics used to classify the actions performed by developers during the development cycle. The heuristics were based on those presented by Fucci et al. [9] and Kou et al. [15].

3.1 Actions

To define each heuristic, it was necessary to classify the actions that are often executed by developers. In Table 2 each action and its respective interpretation are presented. Five essential actions were considered to produce the necessary heuristics to classify each scenario used in the software development cycle. The Test Creation action comprises creating an automated test case, either before or after writing the production code. The Test Pass action refers to the execution of one or more automated test cases successfully. The Test Failure action, contrary to the Test Pass action, is related to the execution of one or more failed automated test cases. The Test Editing action covers the inclusion, change, or removal of source code from existing automated test cases. The Code Editing action, similarly to the Test Editing action, corresponds to the inclusion, modification, and removal of production source code.

Table 2. Development lifecycle actions.

Action	Definition
Test Creation	Characterized by the creation of automatic test cases
Test Pass	Characterized by the execution of test cases that result in success
Test Failure	Characterized by running test cases that result in failure
Test Editing	Characterized by adding, changing or removing code from test cases
Code Editing	Characterized by adding, changing or removing production source code

3.2 Categories

For the development of the Butterfly tool, the heuristics underwent changes, as presented in Table 3. To define the heuristics it was necessary to evaluate in detail the life cycle of each development. The new heuristic model consists of 6 categories and 16 types of episodes. For this new model, the Production category was removed and a new category was added, called Test Driven Development. In this new category you can evaluate the entire red-green-refactoring life cycle of TDD. Like the other tools, Butterfly also considers the end of the development cycle as the Test Pass action. The tool includes the following categories: Test Addition (TA), Test-first (TF), Test-last (TL), Refactoring (RF), Test Driven Development (TDD) and Unknown (UK).

Table 3. Heuristics used to infer the classification of the development cycle.

Type	Definition
Test Addition	TA1. Test Creation → Test Pass
	TA2. Test Creation → Test Failure → Test Editing → Test Pass
Test-first	TF1. Test Creation → Code Editing → Test Pass
	TF2. Test Creation → Test Failure → Code Editing → Test Pass
	TF3. Test Creation → Code Editing → Test Failure → Code Editing → Test Pass
Test-last	TL1. Code Editing → Test Creation → Test Pass
	TL2. Code Editing → Test Creation → Test Failure → Test Editing → Test Pass
Refactoring	RF1. Code Editing → Test Pass
	RF2. Code Editing → Test Failure → Code Editing → Test Pass
	RF3. Test Editing → Test Pass
	RF4. Test Editing → Test Failure → Test Editing → Test Pass
Test Driven Development	TDD1. Test Creation → Test Failure → Code Editing → Test Pass
	TDD2. Test Creation → Test Failure → Code Editing → Test Pass → Test Editing → Test Pass
	TDD3. Test Creation → Test Failure → Code Editing → Test Pass → Test Editing → Test Failure → Test Editing → Test Pass
	TDD4. Test Creation → Test Failure → Code Editing → Test Pass → Code Editing → Test Failure → Code Editing → Test Pass
Unknown	UK1. None of the above → Test pass

Test Addition. It is understood by the addition of new test cases. In this category there is no change in production source code, only in test source code. The possible flows are seen in the Fig. 1. The first flow corresponds to a test case which was added and that did not fail when executed. The second flow considers that, after adding the test case, it failed and had to be edited until eventually passing.

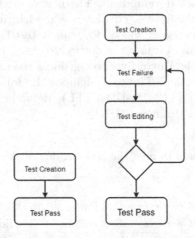

Fig. 1. Test addition flows.

Test-First. In this category, the test case must be created before the corresponding production code. The possible flows are demonstrated in Fig. 2. The first scenario considers that, after test case and code creation, the test case passed. In the second scenario, the test case is created and executed (probably due to the absence of the corresponding production code), then the production code is edited until the test case finally pass. The third flow is similar to the second, but without the execution of the test case just after its creation.

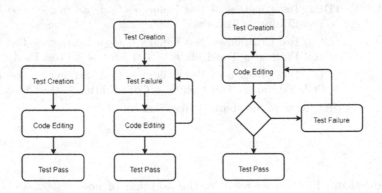

Fig. 2. Test-first flows.

Test-Last. In this category, the test case must be created after the production code is created. The possible flows are demonstrated in Fig. 3. In the first flow, production code and test code are created and the test case pass. In the second flow, the test case fails, which requires further modification of the tests until it eventually pass.

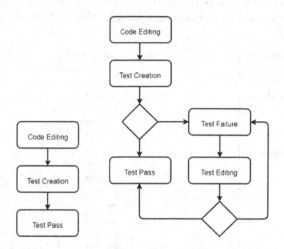

Fig. 3. Test-last flows.

Refactoring. In this category, it can be performed refactoring for production or test source code. It also comprehends activities associated with the improvement of the source code, whether it is carried out in the production code or in test cases. The possible flows are presented in Fig. 4. Two flows are associated with production code improvement, where test cases can pass after code editing or, in

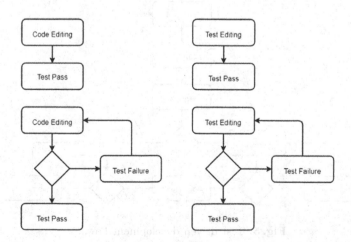

Fig. 4. Refactoring flows.

case of failure, further code editing is required. Respectively, there are two flows associated with test case improvement, where test cases are under modification.

Test Driven Development. In this category, it must be performed the test case creation before creating production source code. After the production code is created, it is necessary to perform the refactoring of the production and test source code. The possible flows are presented in Fig. 5. The first flow represents

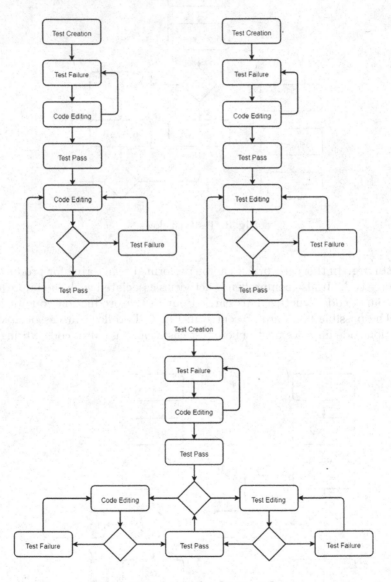

Fig. 5. Test driven development flows.

the traditional TDD cycle, in which test case is created, it fails, production code is created and modified until the test case pass, and code is improved (by refactoring), always considering the results of test cases execution. In the second flow, instead of improving the production code, the code for test cases is improved (for instance, considering a coverage criteria). Finally, the third flow is a combination of the both, improving production code and test cases.

Unknown. In order for this category to be classified by the tool, none of the known categories is achieved. In this way, everything that does not contemplate the heuristics of Table 3 will be classified as Unknown.

3.3 Environment

The tool can be used by developers who use the Eclipse Integrated Development Environment (IDE), which is compatible with the Oxygen and Photon versions. It requires Java Runtime Environment (JRE) and Java Development Kit (JDK) in version 8 or higher. The tool for running the automatic tests should be version 4 or higher of JUnit. The Butterfly tool is available on Github[1].

4 Case Study

To evaluate the tool the GQM (Goals, Questions and Metrics) paradigm was used. It consists of a mechanism to define and evolve a set of objectives using metrics [1]. According to some authors, the GQM approach is recommended for the definition of experimental studies [14, 21] (Table 4).

Table 4. GQM - goals, questions and metrics.

Goals	Questions	Metrics
G1: Evaluate the compliance of the TDD process within iterative software development	Q1. Is it possible to sort the actions of the episodes in the categories of Test-addition, Test-first, Test-last, Test driven development, Refactoring, and Unknown?	M1. Number of classifications M2. Number of actions M3. Number of unit tests M4. Test coverage

---

[1] https://github.com/altitdb/butterfly.

4.1   Instrumentation

The development environment used by the participants has Java in version 8, IDE Eclipse Oxygen and JUnit 4. The results were generated by the Butterfly tool installed in the participants Eclipse. Each participant was responsible for sending the project data created during the experiment. The application chosen for development was the Bowling Game, which is often used for studies regarding TDD. The Bowling Game is responsible for calculating the score of a player in a bowling game according to the requirements specified in Table 5.

Table 5. Bowling game requirements.

R1	The score of the game can be consulted at any time
R2	The game consists of 10 rounds
R3	The player is entitled to two shots to reach the maximum score (10) on each round
R4	If on the first shot the maximum score is reached (strike), the player will not be entitled to the second shoot
R5	If in both shot the maximum score is reached (spare), the player will have as bonus the score obtained in the next move
R6	The strike score bonus is the value of the next two moves
R7	The player will have two extra shots if he strikes in the tenth round
R8	If he reaches the spare in the two shots after the tenth round, the player will be entitled to one extra shot

4.2   Subjects

The study was attended by professionals working in an organization focused on software development for the financial market with about 450 professionals in the area of Information Technology (IT). Among the professionals, 7 (seven) participated. Participants belong to a team of professionals who have completed advanced IT courses, such as Systems Analysis and Development, Computer Science, Information Systems, Computer Science and Software Engineering. They perform the role of Systems Analyst within the organization and are knowledgeable with Java language, Eclipse development IDE, test automation tools and TDD.

4.3   Execution

The execution was organized in three phases: (i) installation and training of the Butterfly tool, (ii) development of the Bowling Game and (iii) sending the results. In phase (i), the professionals installed the tool in the Eclipse IDE and received the training to learn how the tool should be handled. In phase (ii) the professionals developed the Bowling Game using the Java language, test tool JUnit and TDD. For each Bowling Game requirement, it is expected that a set of development activities are performed, from which the development cycles can be detected. No minimum or maximum time was set for the development of the game. In phase (iii) the professionals sent the developed game and the results to the authors by email for evaluation.

5 Results

Considering the purpose of this study, a new tool, called Butterfly, was developed. It is an evolution of Besouro tool (which, in turn, was an evolution of the Zorro tool). The main differences, as shown in Table 6, are related to compliance verification with respect to TDD and implementation dependencies.

Table 6. Comparison of automatic TDD recognition systems.

Tool	Dependencies	Compliance	User feedback	Compliance report
Zorro [15]	Hackystat, SDSA, Jess	Context-sensitive compliance	No	No
Besouro [4]	Listeners, JESS, VCS	Varying, according to the implemented component	Yes	No
Butterfly	Listeners, VCS	Standard implementation according to pre-established heuristics	Yes	Yes

The tool developed in this study aims to measure compliance and evaluate the TDD life cycle, which was limited or not possible using in other tools. Butterfly allows to check whether the developer is using TDD correctly, or if is only using TDD phases such as Test-first and Refactoring. Considering the features from Table 6, the following differences can be highlighted:

- Dependencies: In the previous tools, some dependencies were fundamental to the operation of the tool. For instance, the Jess tool was one of the main components required by them, but it was not free for commercial use. This led to its removal from the Butterfly tool, replacing its functionality by new code written by the authors.
- Compliance: Actions described in the literature were considered, and it no longer varies according to contexts or implementations as performed in the previous tools.
- User feedback: It was kept as in the Butterfly tool, given its importance in classifying actions that are not considered correct, making it possible to improve the tool in the future.
- Compliance report: A novelty in the Butterfly tool is the summarization of the actions performed by the user. With this report it is possible to analyze the percentage of use of the user's actions.

A case study was conducted to validate the use of the developed tool. In Table 7, it is presented a summary of the measurements taken from the executions for each developer during the execution of the empirical study described in Sect. 4. For metrics, the following definitions are adopted: classifications (M1) as the number of episodes classified by the tool according to the categories defined in Table 3; actions (M2) as the amount of actions carried out by each developer, as presented in Table 2; unit tests (M3) as the amount of automated test cases created by the developers; and test coverage (M4) as the percentage of production code that was covered by the unit tests with respect to control-flow criterion (statements coverage).

Table 7. Measurements regarding usage of Butterfly tool.

Developer	Classifications (M1)	Actions (M2)	Unit tests (M3)	Test coverage (M4)
D1	38	311	12	92
D2	32	223	6	**100**
D3	**63**	**692**	**21**	90.6
D4	**88**	**505**	13	**99.7**
D5	35	356	10	96.2
D6	**119**	**732**	**29**	95.2
D7	21	262	10	**100**
Average	56.57	440.14	14.42	96.24
Median	38	356	12	96.2

Metrics M1 and M2 are directly linked to the activity development effort while metrics M3 and M4 can be used to diagnose testing activities. Comparing the measurements with manual analysis of the code produced by the developers, There is no disagreement with the measurements (and classifications) made by the tool against the actions carried out by the user.

6   Discussion

Using the tool, it was possible to evaluate the TDD life cycle, evaluating the red-green-refactoring cycle as a whole and separately. The granularity, uniformity, sequence and effort of refactoring, which were presented in the Table 1, can be measured individually or in combination. Furthermore, providing facilities that can summarize the results generated by users actions facilitates the analysis of long-term empirical studies or with a large amount of user participation. Therefore, the tool enable to further evaluate development activities, and to try out new approaches within each process of the TDD life cycle, being able to evaluate the effects within a single TDD phase or for the complete TDD iteration. For instance, the inclusion of the use of test criteria in the TDD cycle is being evaluated, and this study provides a tool that will help evaluate this inclusion, so that gains are obtained and threats removed or mitigated.

Making the tool open-source gives researchers the possibility of new implementations without the need to learn new frameworks. In order for the extensibility of the tool to be carried out, only knowledge in the Java language is necessary.

7 Conclusion

In this study, it was presented the Butterfly tool, which is a tool built with the purpose of analyzing the process of developing iterative software by classifying it into categories. Each category has a set of heuristics, which are responsible for determining in which category the user's actions meet. The categories offered by the tool are: Test Addition, Test-first, Test-last, Test Driven Development, Refactoring, and Unknown.

To perform the tool evaluation the GQM paradigm was used, allowing to elaborate objectives, questions and metrics for the purpose of evaluating experimental studies. The Butterfly tool serves the purpose of this study, which is to evaluate the compliance of the TDD process in the development of iterative software. With the established metrics it is possible to verify that the actions and episodes generated were categorized in an expected way. There were no divergences between developers and the categorization performed by the tool.

Finally, a tool that can support empirical studies about TDD was developed, easing the analysis of the information generated. The Butterfly tool was provided on Github[2], so that the source code can be used by researchers or by the community at large. The tool is also open to further improvements, and the community can contribute using the open source format.

References

1. Basili, V.R.: Software modeling and measurement: the goal/question/metric paradigm. Technical report CS-TR-2956, UMIACS-TR-92-96, p. 24. University of Maryland, College Park, MD, USA, September 1992. http://www.cs.umd.edu/~basili/publications/technical/T78.pdf
2. Beck, K.: eXtreme Programming Explained: Embrace Change. Addison-Wesley, Boston (1999)
3. Beck, K.: Test-Driven Development: By Example. Addison-Wesley Professional, Boston (2002)
4. Becker, K., de Souza Costa Pedroso, B., Pimenta, M.S., Jacobi, R.P.: Besouro: a framework for exploring compliance rules in automatic TDD behavior assessment. Inf. Softw. Technol. **57**, 494–508 (2015)
5. Briand, L., Bianculli, D., Nejati, S., Pastore, F., Sabetzadeh, M.: The case for context-driven software engineering research: generalizability is overrated. IEEE Softw. **34**(5), 72–75 (2017)

---

[2] https://github.com/altitdb/butterfly.

6. Causevic, A., Punnekkat, S., Sundmark, D.: TDD^{HQ}: achieving higher quality testing in test driven development. In: Euromicro Conference Series on Software Engineering and Advanced Applications, pp. 33–36, Santander, Spain (2013)

7. Causevic, A., Sundmark, D., Punnekkat, S.: Factors limiting industrial adoption of test driven development: a systematic review. In: International Conference on Software Testing, Verification and Validation, pp. 337–346. IEEE, Berlin, Germany (2011)

8. Causevic, A., Shukla, R., Punnekkat, S., Sundmark, D.: Effects of negative testing on TDD: an industrial experiment. In: Baumeister, H., Weber, B. (eds.) XP 2013. LNBIP, vol. 149, pp. 91–105. Springer, Heidelberg (2013). https://doi.org/10.1007/978-3-642-38314-4_7

9. Fucci, D., Erdogmus, H., Turhan, B., Oivo, M., Juristo, N.: A dissection of the test-driven development process: does it really matter to test-first or to test-last? Trans. Softw. Eng. **43**(7), 597–614 (2017)

10. Garousi, V., Felderer, M., Kuhrmann, M., Herkiloglu, K.: What industry wants from academia in software testing?: Hearing practitioners' opinions. In: International Conference on Evaluation and Assessment in Software Engineering, pp. 65–69. ACM, Karlskrona, Sweden (2017)

11. George, B., Williams, L.: A structured experiment of test-driven development. Inf. Softw. Technol. **46**(5), 337–342 (2004)

12. Hammond, S., Umphress, D.: Test driven development: the state of the practice. In: Smith, R.K., Vrbsky, S.V. (eds.) ACM Annual Southeast Regional Conference, pp. 158–163. ACM, Tuscaloosa, Alabama, USA (2012)

13. Janzen, D., Saiedian, H.: Test-driven development concepts, taxonomy, and future direction. Computer **38**(9), 43–50 (2005)

14. Juristo, N., Moreno, A.M.: Basics of Software Engineering Experimentation. Kluwer Academic Publishers, Dordrecht (2001)

15. Kou, H., Johnson, P.M., Erdogmus, H.: Operational definition and automated inference of test-driven development with Zorro. Ann. Softw. Eng. **17**(1), 57–85 (2010)

16. Offutt, J.: Why don't we publish more TDD research papers? Softw. Test. Verif. Reliab. **28**(4), e1670 (2018)

17. Pachulski Camara, B.H., Graciotto Silva, M.A.: A strategy to combine test-driven development and test criteria to improve learning of programming skills. In: Technical Symposium on Computing Science Education, pp. 443–448. ACM, Memphis, TN, USA (2016)

18. Raulamo-Jurvanen, P., Mäntylä, M., Garousi, V.: Choosing the right test automation tool: a grey literature review of practitioner sources. In: International Conference on Evaluation and Assessment in Software Engineering, pp. 21–30. ACM, Karlskrona, Sweden (2017)

19. Shelton, W., Li, N., Ammann, P., Offutt, J.: Adding criteria-based tests to test driven development. In: International Conference on Software Testing, Verification and Validation, pp. 878–886. IEEE, Montreal, QC, Canada (2012)

20. Spinellis, D.: State-of-the-art software testing. IEEE Softw. **34**(5), 4–6 (2017)

21. Wohlin, C., Runeson, P., Höst, M., Ohlsson, M.C., Regnell, B., Wesslén, A.: Experimentation in Software Engineering: An Introduction. Kluwer Academic Publishers, Sweden (2000)

Evaluation of an Agile Maturity Model: Empirical Evidences for Agility Assessments

Adriana Corrêa Rodrigues and Rafaela Mantovani Fontana[✉]

Federal University of Paraná, UFPR,
R. Dr. Alcides Vieira Arcoverde, 1225, Curitiba, PR 81520-260, Brazil
{adriana.rodrigues,rafaela.fontana}@ufpr.br

Abstract. Software process reference models (such as Capability Maturity Model Integration – CMMI–DEV) have been used for years for software process evaluation and improvement. However, when a team uses agile methods for software development, these models hinder sustaining agility in higher maturity levels. This is the reason why some agile maturity models have been proposed in the last years. Although there are some models suggested in literature, few studies actually evaluate these models with real teams. The objective of this study is thus to evaluate an agile maturity model – the Agile Compass – creating empirical results for agile teams in the process improvement field. We conducted this research with two field studies in two different agile teams: an ethnographic study and a focus group. Our findings confirmed the need for empirical validation of academically–proposed models. The Agile Compass was effective in creating a maturity picture for the teams, but both teams seemed to prefer a more "objective" evaluation.

Keywords: Maturity model · Process improvement · Agility assessment · Agile software development

1 Introduction

Maturity models are used in software engineering with the aim to drive software development processes improvement. This improvement means creating products with more quality, in a defined and predictable work process. Currently, the family of standards ISO/IEC 330xx [1] and the Capability Maturity Model Integration for Development (CMMI-DEV) [2] are references to guide improvements in software processes.

When a software development team uses agile methods, development process tend to value – as the Agile Manifesto [3] states – individual and interactions more than processes and tools; working software more than comprehensive documentation; customer collaboration more than contract negotiation and responding to changes more than following a plan. In this context, software improvement initiatives may follow the traditional reference models, but with implications. As

© Springer Nature Switzerland AG 2019
G. S. Tonin et al. (Eds.): WBMA 2018, CCIS 981, pp. 49–62, 2019.
https://doi.org/10.1007/978-3-030-14310-7_4

traditional reference models use process definition and control to reach maturity in software development, it usually implies that agility might be hindered in higher maturity levels [4,5].

Some researchers have been proposing agile maturity models [6,8,10]. These models adapt improvement guidelines to the values and principles stated by agile methods. Although a number of models have been proposed with different structures, only few of them are empirically evaluated [10] and we do not know whether they are applicable in real teams. Even agility assessment models proposed in industry have shown not to be effective on aiding agile adopters to improve their agility [13].

Empirical evaluations, though, are essential for researchers to understand the applicability of the solutions they propose and create agile maturity models that effectively aid improving agility. These models should fit for the purpose of being actually used in industry [11,13].

This study aims at evaluating one of the agile maturity models, the Agile Compass, proposed by Fontana et al. [12]. The Agile Compass is a tool that allows assessing maturity in agile software development teams without the need of extensive process definition and control. It defines agile software development maturity as a set of outcomes that are pursued by teams and the assessment is performed with a check-list and meetings for discussion.

With the general objective of evaluating the Agile Compass, we defined three specific objectives: to evaluate its efficacy to measure maturity, to evaluate the utility of the model and to identify practitioners perceptions. Our results interest to industry practitioners, as we show how to conduct an agility assessment in two different ways. The findings also interest to academics, as we (1) applied two research methods for an agile maturity model evaluation and (2) found evidence about the issues that could be improved for the creation of new and more practical agile maturity models.

This paper is organized as follows: Sect. 2 describes related work and Sect. 3 briefly describes the Agile Compass. Next, Sect. 4 describes our research approach, Sect. 5 describes results and, finally, we discuss findings and conclude the paper.

2   Related Work

Maturity models for agile software development have been proposed for years. More than a dozen models are described by academic works [11] and, in industry, tens of options may be found [7]. However, few of them are created based on empirical work and even less of them have their assessment evaluated academically. It has been a concern in recent works to apply these models in real teams and understand usages and advantages [13].

The evaluation of these models must be performed by in-depth studies, so that assessed teams get observed and empirical results uncovered. The work by Özcan-Top and Demirörs [14], for example, describes the application of the

Software Agility Assessment Model (AgilityMOD). As a result, authors identified some necessary improvements such as redundancies, missing practices, and excess of practices.

The study described by Gren et al. [15] evaluates the Agile Measurement Index (SAMI), proposed by Sidky et al. [16]. The authors found out that, although the SAMI model evaluated agility according to the number of practices adopted, teams use practices that are not related to agile principles and, thus, this measurement may not be valid. They conclude that it is not easy to assess agility with a quantitative measurement and that behavior evaluation might give a better understanding of the agility situation in a team.

The model we chose to evaluate in this study does not provide a quantitative measurement and also does not identifies practices adopted. Next section describes how the Agile Compass [12] assesses agile maturity.

3 The Agile Compass

The Agile Compass is a model created with empirical data from nine different agile teams, as described in Fontana et al. [12]. It defines agile maturity as a search for *outcomes*. Teams may use different practices, techniques and methods to pursue these outcomes.

The assessment is based on the evaluation whether the outcomes were accomplished by the team. Figure 1 shows the outcomes and the categories in which they are organized.

The *practices learning* category comprises outcomes that teams pursue when they decide to change the way they work. The *team conduct* category represents how the team evolves behavior in the use of agile methods. The *deliveries pace* shows how deliveries evolve as the team matures. The *features disclosure* category comprises the outcomes pursued by teams as they evolve the way requirements are elicited. The *software product* category represents the outcomes teams accomplish when they try to improve the software product. The *customer relationship* comprises outcomes pursued by teams when they implement practices to improve their relationship with the customer and, last but not least, the *organizational support*, represents the organization position on respect to agile adoption.

For the assessment, each of these outcomes is described by a statement and by two or three check-list items. The authors [12] propose that team members evaluate together this check-list and discuss which outcomes have been partially or fully accomplished. This discussion may also lead to a plan of action for agility improvement. Figure 1 shows in gray the outcomes accomplished by mature teams and next section describes our research approach to evaluate this assessment method.

4 Research Approach

The objective of this research was to evaluate the Agile Compass as a maturity assessment tool for agile software development teams. This study is a Design

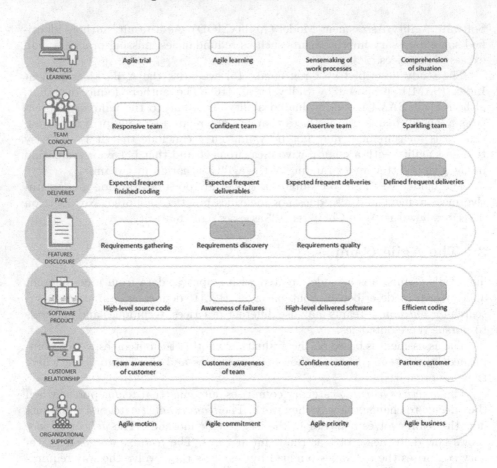

Fig. 1. The Agile Compass outcomes and categories. Adapted from [12].

Science Research (DSR), which one of the objectives is to "evaluate an instanti-ation of a designed artifact to establish its utility and efficacy (or lack thereof) for achieving its stated purpose" [19, p. 425]. The designed artifact is the Agile Compass to be evaluated in an ex-post evaluation in naturalistic settings (clas-sification given by Venable et al. [19]).

Based on the guideline to evaluate efficacy and utility, the specific objectives we defined were:

– Evaluating Agile Compass efficacy on assessing maturity;
– Evaluating Agile Compass utility on assessing maturity; and
– Evaluating team members perception on the tool usage.

We evaluated the Agile Compass Assessment in two teams. The methods chosen to accomplish this objective were, in the first team, the ethnographic study and, in the second team, the focus group.

4.1   The Ethnographic Study

According to Bryman [17] an ethnographic study is an "observation research". When it is in a structured form, comprises "direct observation of behaviour and the recording of that behaviour in terms of categories that have been dived prior to the start of data collection" [17, p. 270]. Our observation in the first team comprised an observation schema in which we watched the Agile Compass Assessment meeting and reported the types of interactions among team members every time it changed (without a fixed timebox). The coding we used were:

1. The team is discussing about the action plan to improve process;
2. The team is discussing whether a specific outcome was accomplished;
3. The team is discussing which practices they use to fill out an outcome;
4. Discussion related to the topic;
5. Discussions *not* related to the topic;
6. Critics among team members;
7. General lack of interest/tiredness/silence/confusion;

The observation schema was based on the suggestions given by Bryman [17] and helped us identifying team behaviour during the assessment, as we did not interfere in the dynamics of the discussions.

After the assessment meeting finished, we asked team members to answer a questionnaire with questions to capture their perceptions about the tool. They evaluated the following statements and marked their opinion, in a 5-point Likert scale ("completely disagree", "partially disagree", "neutral", "partially agree" or "completely agree"):

- For *efficacy* evaluation:
  - The Agile Compass represents effectively what is maturity for agile software development
  - The Agile Compass helps me understanding my team's maturity in agile
  - The Agile Compass enables the comparison of maturity between different teams
- For *utility* evaluation:
  - The Agile Compass helps my team to evolve practices towards maturity
  - The Agile Compass helps my team to evolve behaviours towards maturity
  - I could accomplish the same improvement results in other ways

4.2   The Focus Group

The focus group is a research method that aims at understanding how people feel or think on respect to a matter, an idea, a product or a service [20]. This method comprises five main characteristics: (1) a small group that (2) presents certain properties, (3) that provide qualitative data, (4) in a focused discussion (5) to help understanding a topic of interest.

These properties apply to our study, in the second studied team, in the following way:

1. A software development team;
2. That use agile methods;
3. Which will attend to an Agile Compass Assessment session;
4. Guided and analyzed by the researcher;
5. To identify the tool's efficacy and utility.

The steps for the execution of the focus group were defined according to the work by Romain [21]: Preparation, Phase 1 and Phase 2. Preparation comprised defining the protocol for the study, preparing necessary material (printed Agile Compass check-lists, pens, etc) and setting the meeting schedule with the company. Phase 1 comprised a meeting in which we presented the Agile Compass for team members, explaining each of the categories and outcomes, and each individual filled out an Agile Compass checklist with his own opinion. In Phase 2, we conducted a second meeting – the focus group – when all results from previous phase were compiled, shown to all team members and, in a guided discussion, they arrived to a consensus about the agility assessment. In Phase 2, we also observed discussions using the structured schema described in the ethnographic study, coding team behavior for each 3–5 min.

All meetings were recorded with participants authorization. The recordings were used to remember specific points in the discussions. After the assessment session, we asked team members to fill out the same evaluation form as the ethnographic study, providing us a view of their perception about the tool.

4.3   Threats to Validity

This study is a qualitative research and, as such, presents specific validity and reliability issues [17] that were addressed in our protocol in the following ways. Regarding *external reliability* (the degree to which a study may be replicated), we have based our protocol in scientific method literature and described our research steps. On respect to *internal reliability* (the members of a research may agree with results), we have created research reports after conducting the field studies and presented them to key participants, so that they could verify whether our conclusions met their perceptions.

Regarding *internal validity* (whether there is a good match between researchers' observations and theoretical ideas) and *external validity* (which is the degree to which results may be generalized) we consider further field studies may be performed to confirm or refute our findings.

5   Results

Our study was conducted with two different software development teams. The first team worked in a Brazilian company that develops software for the government sector, with about 1500 employees and 25 years in the market. The team had 6 people. They were already using the Agile Compass to assess maturity in the teams, and we conducted this study in their second assessment session.

For the focus group, we contacted four different companies to perform the study, but only one accepted, which is the second team. They worked in a multinational company with about 2000 employees in Brazil. The team developed configurations in a human resources system, used by the company. The team had 10 people, with 8 of them in Brazil and 2 of them in USA.

Next subsections present the results for each of the studies.

5.1 Agile Compass Observation: Ethnographic Study

As explained in Sect. 4.1, we observed an Agile Compass assessment session. The session took 55 min, was guided by the team's agile coach and we did not interfere in the dynamics of the meeting (only solving some doubts about the tool).

The method for conducting the assessment was created by their agile coach. She created a spreadsheet with the Agile Compass check-list and, for each category, for each outcome, she asked the team whether the check-list item was verified in the team. The whole team responded together and they arrived to a consensus at the time. They did not discuss improvements needed nor plans of action because the company used the Agile Compass exclusively to measure agility adoption.

This is the reason they created indicators. Each check-list item marked had a value of 1. A fully accomplished outcome had a value of 3. Results were plotted in a graphic that allowed the team to visualize its accomplished outcomes and compare with other assessment sessions. Figure 2 shows the graphic created by the team's agile coach. The resulting assessment of the session we observed is in orange line, compared with a previous session, green line, and mature outcomes in blue bars.

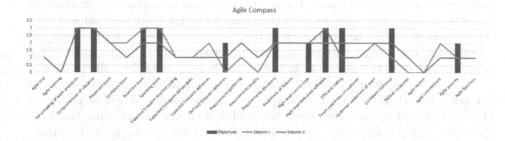

Fig. 2. The result of the Agile Compass assessment in the first team. X axis shows Agile Compass outcomes and Y axis the indicator from 0 to 3. Figure provided by the team's agile coach. (Color figure online)

Figure 2 shows that the team, in the moment of the session, had fully or partially accomplished mature outcomes in the practices learning category and also in the team conduct category (see first eight outcomes in X axis). They were still on the way to get to mature outcomes on deliveries pace, as their deliveries still got late (see next four outcomes). Regarding features discovery – represented by next three outcomes on X axis, the team had partially accomplished the mature outcome (requirements discovery). On respect to software product (next four outcomes), almost all mature outcomes had been accomplished, and for customer relationship and organizational support, mature outcomes had partially been accomplished (last eight outcomes).

As we performed a structured observation, we made notes (using the codes described in Sect. 4.1) to identify how the team used the session time. The team spent 47% of the time with discussions whether an outcome was accomplished; 37% discussing practices they were using; and 4% of the time with related topics. The other 5% was distributed among plan of action, other unrelated topics and lack of interest.

During the observation, we also made notes on the issues discussed. We saw they felt difficulties in understanding some statements in the Agile Compass check-list and that some of the items they felt did not apply to the team (for example, outcomes that they do not have control over, such as organizational support). We also felt some embarrassment when exposing negative situations (such as lack of management support).

On respect to how the team evaluated the Agile Compass session, their responses to our questionnaire are shown in Fig. 3 (one of the team members did not respond). We can observe that the majority of the team believes the Agile Compass represents what is maturity in agile software development, helps understanding team's situation, helps comparison among teams and helps the team to evolve practices and behavior. Nevertheless, they also state that these results could be accomplished with other tools.

Agile Compass Efficacy, Utility and Team's Perception: The findings from ethnographic study have shown that the Agile Compass was effective on allowing the maturity assessment in the team. Although there were some doubts on the statements defined in the check-list, the team arrived to a consensus and could define whether an outcome was accomplished or not. The graphic in Fig. 2 represents the agility assessment in the team. On respect to the utility, we could see the tool being useful to assess maturity, but not to guide improvements, as the team almost did not discuss on how to improve results. When we presented the study report to the agile coach, she said that they were not using the Agile Compass with this objective. They wanted a tool to measure agility and compare teams. On respect to team perception, we observe a positive opinion about the tool, approving its efficacy and utility.

5.2   Agile Compass Application: Focus Group Study

The main characteristic of the focus group is that it is guided by the researcher. Thus, differently from the ethnographic study, we conducted the assessment in this team, as suggested by the Agile Compass authors [12] and as applied in Romain [21].

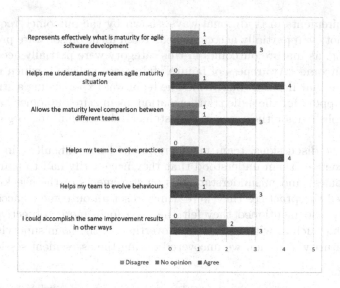

Fig. 3. The evaluation of the first team on the Agile Compass (number of responses).

In a first meeting, we explained the Agile Compass and collected individual team members forms. In these forms, they individually checked out the items from the Agile Compass which they verified in their team. This section took 40 min. We then consolidated all responses in a single spreadsheet, with the same layout as the Agile Compass, as shown in Fig. 4. In each cell (that represents an outcome) we show which team members (P1, P2, P3, ...) marked an item.

In the second meeting, the two members located in USA did not participate. In this session, we presented the spreadsheet with all members responses consolidated and, going through each one, we stimulated a discussion asking why people marked a specific item, whether all the others agreed and, then finally whether the outcome was accomplished. If the team did not see the outcome as accomplished, it was left blank in the spreadsheet. If they agreed the outcome as partially accomplished, it was set in light gray, and, if they found the outcome as fully accomplished, it was filled in dark gray. We set an asterisk in the outcomes considered mature, for the team to have a reference during the discussions. This session took one hour.

The maturity situation of the team, in the moment of the session, is shown in Fig. 4. We see here a team starting the agile transformation. On respect to practices learning, outcomes had partially been accomplished, but discussions showed the team was on the way to improve and fully accomplish them. On respect to team conduct, the team was a "confident team" on the way to be an "assertive team". However, they still presented characteristics of a "responsive team", as this outcome was partially accomplished. Regarding deliveries, they still got late – this is the situation shown by the fully-accomplished outcome "expected frequent deliveries". On respect to features disclosure, the team still defined requirements in traditional ways, shown by the outcome "requirements discovery" not even partially accomplished. Team focus on software product was still maturing, as mature outcomes in this category were partially accomplished (note the outcome "Awareness of failure" fully accomplished, which means the team is aware that needs to improve). The team was experiencing a strong organizational support for the agile transformation, as mature outcomes had already been accomplished for the categories customer relationship and organizational support.

During the discussions, team members pointed out difficulties in filling the check-list (some of them understood that they necessarily had to mark an item for all outcomes) and misunderstandings on statements of the check-list. They also discussed the practices they were using to set an outcome as accomplished or not. They also mentioned they felt the need for a more "objective" way to see the results, such as with indicators. Nevertheless, the team supervisor agreed with the maturity situation we uncovered during the assessment session.

PRACTICES LEARNING	Agile trial P1 P2 P3 P4 P5 P6 P7 P8 P9 P10	Agile learning P2 P3 P4 P5 P1 P6 P7 P8 P9 P10	Sensemaking of work processes* P1 P2 P3 P4 P5 P6 P7 P8 P9 P10	Comprehension of situation* P1 P2 P3 P4 P5 P6 P7 P8 P9 P10
TEAM CONDUCT	Responsive team P1 P2 P3 P4 P5 P6 P7 P8 P9 P10	Confident team P1 P2 P3 P4 P5 P6 P7 P8 P9 P10	Assertive team* P2 P4 P5 P6 P9 P10 P8	Sparkling team* P2 P3 P4 P1 P5 P10
DELIVERIES PACE	Expected frequent finished coding P1 P2 P3 P4 P5 P6 P7 P8 P9 P10	Expected frequent deliverables P1 P2 P3 P4 P8 P9 P10	Expected frequent deliveries P1 P2 P3 P4 P5 P6 P7 P8 P9 P10	Defined frequent deliveries* P3 P5 P7
FEATURES DISCLOSURE	Requirements gathering P1 P2 P3 P4 P5 P6 P7 P8 P10	Requirements discovery* P2 P5 P6 P7 P8 P9 P10	Requirements quality P1 P2 P3 P4 P6 P8 P10	
SOFTWARE PRODUCT	High-level source code* P1 P2 P3 P4 P5 P6 P8 P9 P10	Awareness of failures P1 P2 P3 P4 P5 P6 P7 P8 P9 P10	High-level delivered software* P1 P2 P3 P4 P6 P8 P9 P10	Efficient coding* P1 P2 P3 P4 P6 P8 P9 P10
CUSTOMER RELATIONSHIP	Team awareness of customer P1 P2 P3 P5 P7 P6 P8 P9 P10	Customer awareness of team P2 P3 P1 P5 P6 P7 P8 P9 P10	Confident customer* P1 P2 P3 P4 P5 P6 P8 P9 P10	Partner customer P1 P2 P3 P4 P5 P6 P8 P9 P10
ORGANIZATIONAL SUPPORT	Agile motion	Agile commitment P1 P2 P3 P5 P6 P7 P8 P9 P10	Agile priority* P1 P3 P2 P4 P5 P7 P8 P9 P10	Agile business P6 P7 P8 P10

Fig. 4. Results for the Agile Compass assessment in Team 2.

From the codes we made notes during the structured observation, we have a situation similar to the first team. Most of the time, the team spent discussing whether a result was accomplished (41%). The team also pointed out practices being used (27% of the time). Discussions related to plans of action and related to the topic summed up 14%. We observed critics in the team (1%) and a significant lack of interest (14%).

As in Team 1, we collected team members perceptions on the Agile Compass as a tool for assessing maturity. Only five of the ten team members responded to our survey. Figure 5 shows the results. Most part of the team have no opinion whether the tool represents the maturity in agile software development. They are divided on respect to the efficacy of the tool on helping the team to understand its situation and on the utility to compare different teams. They agree the tool helps evolving team's practices and behavior. We also see they are divided regarding whether they could reach the same assessment results in other ways.

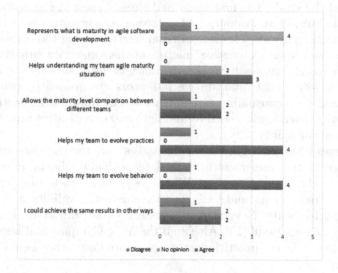

Fig. 5. The evaluation of the second team on the Agile Compass (number of responses).

Agile Compass Efficacy, Utility and Team's Perception: The findings from the focus group have shown that the Agile Compass could provide a maturity picture of the team, but the assessment session needs some improvements, as the team pointed out some check list items they did not understand. Individual evaluations of the tool show that they did not realize their maturity situation, probably because they missed a quantitative indicator. Nevertheless, they found the tool useful to stimulate discussions that may lead to improvements in practices and behavior. The lack of interest during the assessment session probably shows that some team members were not willing to participate in the research.

6   Discussion

The objective of this research was to evaluate the Agile Compass as a maturity assessment tool in agile software development teams. We evaluated Agile Compass assessment sessions in two teams, using two different methods. For the first team, we observed a session conducted by the team, through an ethnographic study. For the second team, we invited them to participate in the research and conducted a focus group for guiding the assessment session.

We found the tool was effective and useful on assessing maturity in the two teams. We could draw a picture of their maturity situation and both teams agreed the tool would help accomplish improvements in agile software development. However both of them missed a quantitative approach to see their maturity situation. Most agile maturity models, as shown in Fontana et al. [11], define their assessment procedures by using quantitative indicators. The Agile Compass approach is qualitative and both teams disliked this subjective approach. When we performed the study, the first team had already created their own "translation" from the subjective evaluation of outcomes to a quantitative indicator, by plotting results in a graph. The second team showed during the discussions that would like to see a more "objective" picture of their maturity situation.

Although recent studies have shown difficulty in quantitatively measuring agility [15], it seems that quantitative indicators are needed by practitioners. Contextual and time-consuming assessments do not full-fill organizations needs [13,15] and we, as academics, need to find light and quantitative ways to provide a measurement for agility [22].

Other issues we observed in these field studies were the language and the procedure defined by the assessment tool. Both teams had doubts on understanding some items in the Agile Compass. When designed artifacts are academically proposed [19], researchers make efforts to evaluate the validity and reliability of their research results. Nevertheless, researches that aim at having practical findings may also be useful [19]. Although the Agile Compass had been academically validated [12], real practitioners usage pointed out other issues that must be considered.

Related work in literature have been confirming the importance of empirically evaluating agile maturity assessment models. Özcan-Top and Demirörs [9,14] evaluate the model they purpose by verifying whether the agility assessment is understood by participants and useful for improvement. They identified their model was effective for its purpose and, as in our work, they also collected the perception of the practitioners on improvements that could be made in the model.

Another evaluation of an agile maturity model is presented by Gren et al. [15]. They, on the other hand, found the evaluated model was not successful on measuring agility. The model they evaluated considered the implementation of practices to evaluate agility and they found it was not useful. They argued that "teams can use agile practices without having them aligned with the agile principles" [15, p. 40] and, thus, practices adoption does not measure agility level. They concluded their study confirming the need to validate current agile maturity models instead of proposing new ones [11,15].

These findings evidence the need for empirical studies validating academically created tools. Even though they have been scientifically tested, these tools need to be refined by practitioners usage, as language and procedures for the assessment are only tested in real settings.

7   Conclusions

This study aimed at evaluating an agile maturity assessment tool – the Agile Compass. Two different teams had their assessment sessions evaluated, using two empirical methods, the ethnographic study and the focus group.

Findings have shown the tool was effective on evaluating team's maturity, but teams still pointed out the need for quantitative indicators for maturity assessment. We also observed the importance of empirical studies to validate academically created tools, to adequate language and usage procedures.

Our results are limited to the teams we studied, as a characteristic of qualitative and in-depth researches [17]. The study protocol should be replicated in other teams with other contexts to confirm or refute our findings.

References

1. ISO/IEC - International Organization for Standardization/ International Electrical Committee. ISO/IEC 33001:2015. Information technology - Process assessment - Concepts and terminology (2015). https://www.iso.org/standard/54175.html. Accessed July 2018
2. CMMI Product Team. CMMI for Development, Version 1.3 (CMU/SEI-2010-TR-033). Software Engineering Institute, Carnegie Mellon University (2010). http://www.sei.cmu.edu/library/abstracts/reports/10tr033.cfm. Accessed July 2018
3. Beck, K., et al.: Manifesto for Agile Software Development (2001). http://agilemanifesto.org/. Accessed July 2018
4. Paulk, M.: Extreme programming from a CMM perspective. IEEE Softw. **18**(6), 19–26 (2001). https://doi.org/10.1109/52.965798
5. Lukasiewicz, K., Miler, J.: Improving agility and discipline of software development with the Scrum and CMMI. IET Softw. **6**(5), 416–422 (2012). https://doi.org/10.1049/ietsen.2011.0193
6. Schweigert, T., Nevalainen, R., Vohwinkel, D., Korsaa, M., Biro, M.: Agile maturity model: oxymoron or the next level of understanding. In: Mas, A., Mesquida, A., Rout, T., O'Connor, R.V., Dorling, A. (eds.) SPICE 2012. CCIS, vol. 290, pp. 289–294. Springer, Heidelberg (2012). https://doi.org/10.1007/978-3-642-30439-2_34
7. Schweigert, T., Vohwinkel, D., Korsaa, M., Nevalainen, R., Biro, M.: Agile maturity model: a synopsis as a first step to synthesis. In: McCaffery, F., O'Connor, R.V., Messnarz, R. (eds.) EuroSPI 2013. CCIS, vol. 364, pp. 214–227. Springer, Heidelberg (2013). https://doi.org/10.1007/978-3-642-39179-8_19
8. Özcan-Top, Ö., Demirörs, O.: Assessment of agile maturity models: a multiple case study. In: Woronowicz, T., Rout, T., O'Connor, R.V., Dorling, A. (eds.) SPICE 2013. CCIS, vol. 349, pp. 130–141. Springer, Heidelberg (2013). https://doi.org/10.1007/978-3-642-38833-0_12
9. Özcan-Top, Ö., Demirörs, O.: A reference model for software agility assessment: agilitymod. In: Rout, T., O'Connor, R.V., Dorling, A. (eds.) SPICE 2015. CCIS, vol. 526, pp. 145–158. Springer, Cham (2015). https://doi.org/10.1007/978-3-319-19860-6_12
10. Leppänen, M.: A comparative analysis of agile maturity models. In: Pooley, R., et al. (eds.) Information Systems Development: Reflections, Challenges and New Directions, pp. 329–343. Springer, New York (2013). https://doi.org/10.1007/978-1-4614-1951-5_27
11. Fontana, R.M., Albuquerque, R., Luz, R., Moises, A.C., Malucelli, A., Reinehr, S.: Maturity models for agile software development: what are they? In: Larrucea, X., Santamaria, I., O'Connor, R.V., Messnarz, R. (eds.) EuroSPI 2018. CCIS, vol. 896, pp. 3–14. Springer, Cham (2018). https://doi.org/10.1007/978-3-319-97925-0_1

12. Fontana, R.M., Reinehr, S., Malucelli, A.: Agile compass: a tool for identifying maturity in agile software-development teams. IEEE Softw. **32**(6), 20–23 (2015). https://doi.org/10.1109/MS.2015.135
13. Adalı, O.E., Özcan-Top, Ö., Demirörs, O.: Evaluation of agility assessment tools: a multiple case study. In: Clarke, P.M., O'Connor, R.V., Rout, T., Dorling, A. (eds.) SPICE 2016. CCIS, vol. 609, pp. 135–149. Springer, Cham (2016). https://doi.org/10.1007/978-3-319-38980-6_11
14. Özcan-Top, Ö., Demirörs, O.: Assessing software agility: an exploratory case study. In: Mitasiunas, A., Rout, T., O'Connor, R.V., Dorling, A. (eds.) SPICE 2014. CCIS, vol. 477, pp. 202–213. Springer, Cham (2014). https://doi.org/10.1007/978-3-319-13036-1_18
15. Gren, L., Torkar, R., Feldt, R.: The prospects of a quantitative measurement agility: a validation study on an agile maturity model. J. Syst. Softw. **107**, 38–49 (2015). https://doi.org/10.1016/j.jss.2015.05.008
16. Sidky, A., Arthur, J., Bohner, S.: A disciplined approach to adopting agile practices: the agile adoption framework. Innov. Syst. Softw. Eng. **3**(3), 203–216 (2007). https://doi.org/10.1007/s11334-007-0026-z
17. Bryman, A.: Social Research Methods, 4th edn. Oxford University Press, New York (2012)
18. Schwartzman, H.B.: Ethnography in Organizations. Qualitative Research Methods Series, vol. 27. Sage Publications, Thousand Oaks (1993)
19. Venable, J., Pries-Heje, J., Baskerville, R.: A comprehensive framework for evaluation in design science research. In: Peffers, K., Rothenberger, M., Kuechler, B. (eds.) DESRIST 2012. LNCS, vol. 7286, pp. 423–438. Springer, Heidelberg (2012). https://doi.org/10.1007/978-3-642-29863-9_31
20. Krueger, R.A.: Focus Groups: A Practical Guide for Applied Research, 5th edn. Sage Publications, Thousand Oaks (2015)
21. Romain, G.: Characterizing the presence of agility in large-scale agile software development. Masters thesis presented in the Faculty of Computer Science of the Pontifical Catholic University of Rio Grande do Sul (PUCRS) (2015)
22. Buglione, L.: Light maturity models (LMM): an Agile application. In: Profes 2011: Proceedings of the 12th International Conference on Product Focused Software Development and Process Improvement (2011)

Strategies to Increase Customer Value in Agile Software Development

Fernando Sambinelli[(⊠)] ⓘ and Marcos A. F. Borges ⓘ

University of Campinas, Limeira, SP 13484-332, Brazil
180172@g.unicamp.br, marcosborges@ft.unicamp.br

Abstract. Nowadays, the software industry is widely applying agile methods. However, while agile principles emphasize the development of software that delivers "customer value" as a key determinant to success in new products and service designs, there are still a few studies that demonstrate how this occurs in practice. In this study, strategies to increase customer value are discussed in literature, especially in the context of Agile Software Development. The results of systematic literature review were validated and added to an industrial inventory. Based on these investigations, 15 strategies to increase customer value have been identified and detailed at the level of approaches, techniques, tools and metrics. The results obtained reinforce the complexity and the need for new empirical studies on the subject, mainly to investigate the key success factors and main challenges for the adoption of these strategies, as well as the positive and negative impacts caused by their implementations in practice.

Keywords: Agile methods · Customer value · Product development

1 Introduction

In the first principle of the Agile Manifesto [1], which represents the fundamental milestone of Agile Software Development (ASD), it is possible to observe the priority given to customer satisfaction through the early and continuous delivery of "valuable software" [2]. Likewise, the Lean Thinking principles, which originated at Toyota and influenced the ASD, point out the need to increase customer value, eliminating the waste of conducting activities or processes that do not generate value [3].

The concept of "value" is referenced in literature as complex, difficult to understand, conceptualize and model [4, 5]. It has different meanings in specific contexts and there are many ways of describing it [6]. Neither is it a static concept, but it evolves constantly and is influenced by the experiences and needs of customers. Despite these challenges, a deeper view of how value is perceived and created would allow these processes to be more effective [7, 8]. The customer value takes into account the perspective of a company's customers, considering what they want and believe to acquire by buying and using a product or service [9].

The primary goal of any business organization is to create customer value. Delivering this value and maintaining the flow of customer value in a sustainable and ever-growing form has been the focus and need of most companies worldwide [10] - including in the software industry [11]. However, the challenges of the practical

© Springer Nature Switzerland AG 2019
G. S. Tonin et al. (Eds.): WBMA 2018, CCIS 981, pp. 63–79, 2019.
https://doi.org/10.1007/978-3-030-14310-7_5

application of strategies to increase customer value are currently present in the development of software with low value and underutilized products [12]. Research has reported, in the context of the introduction of agile methods, in the early 2000s that 64% of user-requested features in internal software development projects (non-commercial products) were never, or rarely, used [13]. In some more recent case studies, wastes of up to 50% of developers' time with activities that did not generate any customer value and the development of functions that were not necessary or of little customer value were identified [14]. In addition, decision-making about which software products are to be implemented in companies are often based on ineffective criteria, such as personal opinion of members of executive committees or influenced by the person with the highest salary [15]. In ASD, despite the priority given to the construction of software delivered by customer value, the agile development processes do not contemplate any specific strategy to follow the delivery results of customer value, allowing each team to choose whether or not to adopt any given strategies to achieve this goal.

Many studies have been published in recent years related to ASD, but their contributions address specific or comparative agile methods with other development processes [16]. However, few studies have been devoted to understanding the concept of customer value in a comprehensive and detailed way in software development [17, 18]. The studies have not yet identified which strategies are used to increase customer value among software development companies that adopt ASD, they only mention the creation of value ASD brings [18]. However, somehow these companies have been practicing and pursuing strategies to extract the maximum possible value from their products and services to their customers, in order to continue existing in an environment of constant market changes and global competition [19].

The research reported in this article was carried out in order to accumulate current knowledge about several strategies to increase customer value in the context of ASD and to identify themes for future research. The question of research (QR) addressed in this work is: *How are the strategies currently practiced in the software market to increase customer value in ASD?* The QR was detailed in three other questions:

- QR1: What are the main characteristics of the strategies to increase the customer value considered by agile software development teams?
- QR2: What are the main approaches, techniques and tools used by agile teams to maximize customer value?
- QR3: What are the customer value metrics in use by agile teams?

The study focused on two main cores: an extensive literature analysis and an industrial inventory. One of the main objectives of the literature analysis was to discover the theoretical models and strategies to increase customer value in software industry. The results of the literature review were systematically evaluated, synthesized and presented [20]. The industrial inventory was based on experience reports presented at the main agile global conferences provided by the Agile Alliance[1]. Thus, the study

---

[1] A global non-profit organization, founded by some of the consignees of the Agile Manifesto as well as some additional people, promoter of international agile conferences and supporter of several initiatives of the agile communities. Website at: http://www.agilealliance.org.

provides extensive knowledge about what the academic (research) is proposing and the current state of these strategies in the industry.

This paper was organized as follows: Sect. 2 is a summary of the main theoretical interpretations for customer value present in literature; in Sect. 3, the research setting is described; Sect. 4 presents the outcomes of the literature analysis and industrial inventory; Finally, in Sect. 5, the results of this study as well as its limitations are discussed.

2 Models of Customer Value

The value management literature organizes the concept of value into two main categories: customer value and stakeholder value [21]. The customer value takes into account the perspective of a company's customers, considering what they want and believe to acquire by buying and using a product or service [9]. The concept of value to stakeholders analyzes the value created by a product or service beyond the limit of the business-to-customer relationship and may also consider: suppliers, shareholders, employees, regulatory agencies and many other stakeholders. These multiple perspectives added to the customer's vision can be analyzed to increase the delivered value [9]. However, the focus on customer value is pointed out as primary and a priority to all stakeholders, since it is the basic premise for developing and maintaining a new product or service [22, 23]. The customer value is the source of all other values [9, 24].

The work of [9], depicted in Fig. 1, synthesizes the theoretical customer value models in three main groups: *value components models* (VCM), *benefit-cost ratio models* (BCM) and *means-ends models* (MEM). In VCM, the main elements used in value studies, according to [25], are classified as follows: value of endearment or "desire", value of exchange and utility value. The author states that each decision to purchase products or services includes one of these values cited, or a combination of all these elements. The estimated value invokes the buyer's desire to own because of the property (exchange value) and the exchange value explains why the product interests the buyer, how and when the buyer will use the product (utility value). The utility value describes the performance and physical characteristics of the product. In VCM, the emphasis of the customer value is on the functions and features that a product or service can offer. An example of VCM known in literature is the Kano Model [26].

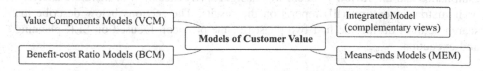

Fig. 1. Theoretical models of CV identified as [9].

In BCM, customer value is defined as the difference between the customer perceptions of benefits received and sacrifices incurred in [27]. Customer benefits include tangible and intangible attributes of the product or service offering, and the sacrifice component includes both monetary and non-monetary factors, such as the time and effort required to acquire and use the product [9], for example. Similarly, [28] defines customer value as the relationship between customer satisfaction and the resources needed to satisfy it. These needs are many and diverse, and a balance is needed between their satisfaction and the resources invested. The fewer the resource used or the greater the satisfaction of the need, the greater the value.

MEMs are based on the assumption that customers acquire and use products or services to achieve favorable ends. This view is prevalent in consumer behavior literature, in particular, in which customer value is defined in terms of personal values, mental images or cognitive representations underlying clients' needs and goals [29]. In MEM theory, according to [27], the links between product attributes, the consequences produced by consumption and the personal values of consumers underlie their decision-making processes. Means are products or services, and ends are personal values considered important to consumers. In MEMs, a product or service represents "a complex set of value satisfactions" for buyers, who attribute value to the product or service according to the perceived ability to meet their needs [30]. Another important point of interpretation in the MEM is that the customer value that matters most is the value in the customer's experience and not the value in the product [31–33]. Several researchers argue that the resulting customer experience is the essence of value proposition [34].

In addition to the three fundamental groups of customer value models, which have been described by [9], there are at least three complementary viewpoints from which customer value might be interpreted, namely: the value exchange model [35], the value buildup model [36, 37] and the dynamics of customer value [38]. None of these different complementary views is able to reflect the richness and complexity of the customer value itself, so [9] propose a integrated model of these complementary groupings in order to give more freedom in the bid value decision.

3　Research Setting

The processes of literature analysis and industrial inventory were based on the guidelines of [20] for performing systematic literature review (SLR), with two researchers conducting these processes. A review protocol was designed to guide the work and consists of three phases: (I) review planning in which objectives were established and the review protocol was designed; (II) execution of literature analysis, or industrial inventory; (III) reports on the results. The sections below describe the search settings during the first two phases of the protocol, focused on SLR planning and execution.

3.1　Literature Analysis

The literature analysis study presented here is focused on bringing together current knowledge on strategies to increase customer value in the context of the ASD.

To ensure the relevance and validity of the results, research was carried out in studies published during the years 2012–2017. The search was conducted using six electronic multidisciplinary databases specialized in the field of computer science and business administration: ABI/Inform (ProQuest), Academic Search Premier (EBSCO), Emerald Journals (Emerald), Science Direct (Elsevier), ACM, and IEEE Xplore. Table 1 shows the search terms and electronic databases used in the literature analysis. Key words related to customer value were used: value creation, business value and customer value. In terms of the search we chose to execute two search strings, one that used a generic term for ASD ("agile") and another containing the specific variations of the main agile methods such as "scrum" and "extreme programming". The term "lean" was applied and considered as an option of variation of agile method in order to cover possible differences of theoretical interpretation between Lean Software Development and ASD [39, 40]. We did not search for studies such as prefaces, article summaries, general presentations, interviews, short articles, special presentations or tutorials: these were excluded from the analysis.

Table 1. Search terms and databases for SLR.

Termos de Busca	Base de Dados
(*'value creation'* OR *'business value'* OR *'customer value'*) AND (*agile* AND *'software development'*)	ABI/Inform (ProQuest)
	Academic Search Premier (EBSCO)
(*'value creation'* OR *'business value'* OR *'customer value'*) AND (*'scrum'* OR *'extreme programming'* OR *'lean'* OR *'crystal'* OR *'feature driven development'* OR *'dynamic systems development'* OR *'adaptive software development'* OR *'kanban'*) AND (*'software development'*)	Emerald Journals (Emerald)
	Science Direct (Elsevier)
	ACM
	IEEE Xplore

A data extraction form is designed to collect individual information from studies. Ten criteria for quality selection and evaluation were also created to ensure the adequate quality of the studies that were finally included in the research material. Examples of inclusion criteria are: study focus, date of publication and clarity of results. The quality assessment generated a score based on the following items: description of the objective and context, research projects, data collection and analysis, justification of findings and conclusions, applicability of results, reduction of threats and use of references. The quality assessment forms were modified for different types of study included in the analysis: quantitative empirical studies, qualitative empirical studies, non-empirical studies and experience reports.

The steps applied to the literature review process are summarized in Fig. 2. A total of 79 studies were evaluated, of which 60 were accepted and included in the research material. The rest of the studies were excluded from the research material because they did not exceed the minimum quality threshold (at least half of the maximum score in the quality assessment). After applying all inclusion and exclusion criteria, 16 journal articles and conference articles were considered relevant as they focused on strategies to increase customer value in the ASD. No experience reports were identified.

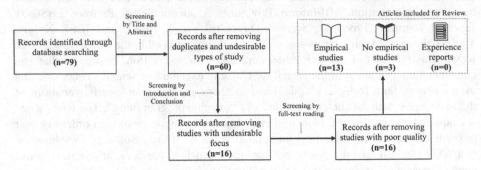

Fig. 2. Steps for literature review process.

3.2   Industrial Inventory

The industrial inventory focused on gaining a better understanding of the adoption of strategies to increase customer value in the ASD and to identify how these strategies are implemented in practice. To achieve these objectives, a secondary data analysis was performed on a set of experience reports in which the application of the strategies to increase customer value in the ASD is clearly evident.

To obtain the necessary secondary data, the related experience reports published at major agile conferences between 2012 and 2017 (including the XP Conference and Agile Conference series) that are publicly available online by the Agile Alliance were collected. The keyword "value" was used as the search term. This more generic form of the term was chosen because of the lack of a more robust search engine in the Agile Alliance's work base, which allowed for the concatenation of terms and operators. This strategy resulted in a larger sum of identified work than would likely occur if the search engine allowed more specific filters. However, this did not affect the final result of this survey. It only increased the necessary work effort.

As in the literature analysis, a data extraction form is designed to collect information individually, from the reports. Selection and evaluation criteria were also created to ensure the appropriate quality of the experience reports that were finally included in the research material. Inclusion criteria were, for example, study focus, date of publication, and clarity of results. The quality assessment included the following items: description of the objective and context; set of observations; analysis of observations; justification of the findings and conclusions; applicability of results and use of references.

The steps for analyzing the secondary data based on experience reports are described in Fig. 3. In the search process, 78 experience reports were identified. After applying the inclusion and exclusion criteria, including quality assessment, 8 agile conference experience reports were found to be relevant because they focused on the proposed scope for this industrial inventory and were therefore included as secondary studies for analysis.

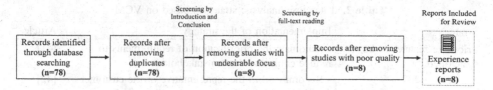

Fig. 3. Steps for literature review process in experience reports.

4 Results

In this section, we present the strategies to increase customer value in the ASD found in literature analysis and in the industrial inventory. The synthesis of the components of these strategies was organized in three subdivisions: characteristics of strategies; approaches, techniques and tools; and customer value metrics.

4.1 Characteristics of Strategies

The theoretical models of value definition contain a broad set of perspectives on this subject. The three fundamental groupings of these models, proposed by [9] and described in Sect. 2, are used to interpret the main characteristics of strategies to increase customer value. They are observed, directly or indirectly, in all articles selected for this study. The strategies identified, in some cases, may be associated with more than one theoretical model. The model to which it was more associated was chosen.

Table 2 summarizes a first set of papers identified in the literature analysis, which use the VCM perspective to justify and interpret customer value [41–46]. In this way, it is the functionalities of the software that have the customer value. They are the ones that will awaken in the customer the desire to have that product or service. It will be for them that the value of exchange and utility will be evaluated. Therefore, the prioritization of software requirements has to play a key role as a strategy to increase customer value. Only product features that have the highest customer value must be developed or at least should be built before the lower value functionalities. Consequently, the planning of releases for software versions should consider this order of priority. On the other hand, the challenges to achieve this goal are mainly in the interdependencies of the requirements and the teams involved in building the solution. In addition, the dissemination of project measurement information is described by [46] as fundamental to promote in the customers a greater awareness of the products and to empower the software development teams, through the increase of transparency, resulting in the increase of the customer value of the products created.

The interpretive basis of customer value in the BCMs considers in particular the relationship between the benefits perceived by customers and the costs (or sacrifices) needed to obtain them. They appear in a second group of literature analysis articles [14, 47–50], which are described in Table 3. The papers discuss strategies and approaches to planning and managing the benefits and costs of software products. They describe

Table 2. Literature analysis: strategies based on VCM.

Strategy	Implementation of the strategy	Article
Prioritize features to be developed	- Automate the prioritization of requirements to reduce conflicts between stakeholders	[41]
	- Recommend to the representative of the customer (product owner) a functional prioritization that reduces the interdependence between the requirements	[42]
	- Team should seek to understand the technical dependencies and risks associated with each functionality, relate the guidelines obtained by a previous business plan, consider the context of outsourcing, and then plan for development	[43]
Plan the roadmapping considering value	- Multifunctional team must prioritize the functionalities of software versions based on a deep understanding of customer needs, not strictly the product, and a long-term vision	[44]
Reduce dependencies between multiple teams	- Team must seek synchronization between teams and product optimizations that reduce cycle time for the customer	[45]
Increase the visibility of products and services	- By disseminating information on project measurements, promoting customer awareness and empowering development teams	[46]

ways of measuring the benefits, especially the natural difficulty of quantifying them, and discuss some cultural changes necessary to make concern about customer value relevant to organizations [47].

Table 3. Literature analysis: strategies based on BCM.

Strategy	Implementation of the strategy	Article
Seeking to maximize the result of the relation between benefit and cost	- Strictly quantify benefits, not just costs	[48, 49]
	- Improve efficiency in cost management	[14]
Consider in organizational performance assessments the value created for customers through the products	- Promote together with leadership a change in the organizational culture on the perception of how value is created	[47]
Seek increased client satisfaction	- Junction of the organizational culture of agility and maturity of processes	[50]

Finally, in the last grouping of the literature analysis are the works aligned with the MEM perspective [51–54]. MEMs are based on the assumption that customers purchase and use products or services to achieve favorable ends. Thus, a product or service represents a complex set of value satisfactions for buyers who attribute value to the product or service according to the perceived ability to meet their needs in their context of use. In this group of literature analysis articles, continuous experimentation is present in all works as a strategy to increase customer value. Continuous experimentation refers to constant testing of the value of products as an integral part of the development process in order to produce more customer value. In this approach, product features are viewed as hypotheses to be tested by experimentation with customers.

The work of [16] uses the Software Value Map (SVM) developed by [55] to understand how agile teams and product owners interpret and prioritize value in development projects. In the SVM, the elements of the VCM are present, such as, to cite a similar case, the valorization of functionalities and non-functional requirements, as well as the elements of the BCM such as, in a similar way, the revenues and costs of the product, hedonic and competitiveness. [16] used sixteen aspects of value to represent four perspectives of value, not restricting the view of the client. The researchers concluded that "delivering the project on schedule" is the highest priority aspect in the ASD. However, depending on the market segment, the value order of priority may change. In this study, the users were not consulted, which could bring a greater understanding on this topic. Table 4 describes the characteristics of the strategies based on MEM and SVM identified in the papers selected for analysis of the literature.

Table 4. Literature analysis: strategies based on MEM and SVM.

Strategy	Implementation of the strategy	Article
Apply continuous cycles of experimentation and learning to find out what customers want. (MEM)	- Collect feedbacks directly from customers. Observe the application usage by customers	[52]
	- Flexible the productive process to accommodate changes resulting from the feedbacks of use of the applications. Monitor the technological and behavioral changes of the client	[51]
	- Seek to know deeply the customers and the domain of the application. Find suitable metrics for customer value	[54]
	- Make decision about product aimed at data and information	[53]
Focus on the most important aspects of value for the customer's market segment. (SVM)	- Identify the most important value aspects and apply the most relevant agile practices to enable them. Be aware that the customer value of software can be interpreted by the team differently from the client	[16]

The selected experience reports present some characteristics and implementations on strategies to increase customer value in the ASD. The three theoretical models groups proposed by [9], VCM, BCM, and MEM, could be identified in the studies

[56–59] as was also found in the literature review. Table 5 describes the strategies identified. In some reports, highlighted in Table 6, however, the strategies relate the implementation of the people management [60], project management [61, 62] and strategic management [63] with the increase in customer value.

Table 5. Experience reports: approaches to increase customer value.

Theory	Strategy	Implementation of the strategy	Article
VCM	Prioritize the most useful features to be developed and validated frequently by the client	- The team should apply the Lean Thinking principles associated with some agile techniques to assist in the prioritization of the functionalities	[56]
BCM	Seek the maximum functional and non-functional quality of the product, without leaving aside, the management of the invested resources	- Project leaders must consistently perform product requirement management	[57]
MEM	Apply continuous cycles of experimentation and learning to find out what customers want	- Collecting of feedbacks directly from customers. Observe the application usage by customers	[58]
		- Conduct continuous product experimentations guided by single value propositions	[59]

A new grouping was suggested to classify and analyze some experience reports: managerial emphasis. All of them share the idea of applying management as a means of increasing customer value. In Table 6 are grouped the experience reports that evidenced the managerial emphasis to increase the customer value. The report [61] comments on the lessons learned from the introduction of a pre-project phase, applied during the sales process that resulted in greater project management effectiveness and, consequently, increased customer value. Improvement in project management, as a means to maximize customer value, is also cited by [62], which describes the effects of Kanban technique application and related metrics. [60] reports on some experiments conducted to study the consequences of frequent and planned changes to the members of agile teams, named by the author as dynamic reteam. According to the report, there was a positive effect on the increase of the motivation of the people and in the organizational learning and, consequently, they were able to increase the customer value of the products. In the experience report of [63], the creation of a visibility room and a structured project monitoring and review process resulted in a better strategic alignment of demands and an increase in product customer value.

Table 6. Experience reports: managerial emphasis as strategy to increase customer value.

Theory	Strategy	Implementation of the strategy	Article
Project management	Improve the efficiency of project management (time, cost and scope)	- Introduce a pre-project phase, involving the potential customer and the development team to improve the efficiency of project management. The new phase seeks to explain ASD to the potential customer, "discover the product" and understand the "psychology" of the customer. Improved project management results in increased customer satisfaction and, consequently, increases the customer value	[61]
	Improve predictability and productivity	- Cycle time management and reduction of work in progress increases the delivered customer value and speed of delivery	[62]
People management	Increase the motivation of development team members and organizational learning	- The customer value of software products is made feasible and improved through motivated and constantly learning people	[60]
Strategic management	Increase the strategic alignment of software development projects	- The strategic alignment of all the company's projects maximizes the customer value	[63]

4.2 Approaches, Techniques and Tools

From the literature analysis and from the industrial inventory, the results could be summarized using a high-level perspective in relation to the approaches, techniques, and tools used by the strategies to increase customer value in the context of the ASD. Figure 4 shows a mental map with the organization of articles and experience reports by the value definition models proposed by [9] and by the conceptual emphases of the approaches, techniques and tools identified.

Figure 4 shows that agile techniques, ceremonies, or artifacts, in their classic forms or adaptations, are recommended in all value definition models. Depending on the objective pursued by the strategy, specific agile techniques or rituals are used as a priority, for example in MEM strategies, the importance of short development cycles (sprints) to obtain user feedback is reinforced [51, 54]. Among the strategies associated with BCM, the agile splitting user stories technique was used to factorize the requirements in order to facilitate the prioritization of the higher customer value functionalities [42]. This finding, on one hand, corroborates with the results of the study [16] that found out that there is a variable influence of each agile practice in relation to the increase in customer value. On the other hand, they are always associated with other techniques and tools that are not classified as agile or, in some cases, adaptations of classical agile practices [45]. Some techniques of Lean Thinking were found among the works, among them, for example, Kanban [62], map value flow [56] and minimum feasible product [52, 59].

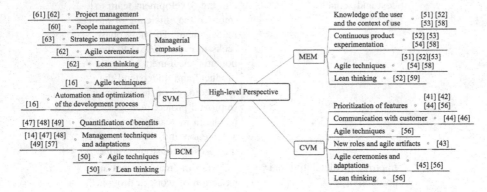

Fig. 4. Map of approaches, techniques and tools identified

4.3   Customer Value Metrics

Some metrics to quantify the customer value were found in literature analysis and industrial inventory concentrated on few publications. A total of 20 metrics were summarized and detailed in relation to their objectives in Table 7. The metrics found are derived from the strategies proposed in these publications. Therefore, in some cases, they may be associated with more than one theoretical model. The model more strongly associated with each strategy was chosen. The articles related to the MEM emphasized the importance of the metrics, mainly, to help in the interpretation of the experiments in their use of the products by the consumers, that is, the value recognized by them. However, the work was not explicit in indicating which metrics were employed. In Table 7 we used the metric identification structure of the Goal-Question-Metric approach [64] to give greater clarity of the objectives of each metric proposed by the respective authors.

In most of the selected experience reports, as was found in the literature analysis, no customer value metrics were found. Only two reports [61, 62], which emphasized the improvement of project management as a strategy to increase customer value, report metrics inherent to the managerial approach given by the authors. [61] indirectly describe time and cost control without citing specific metrics. The author indicates the volume of functionality delivered to the client as a project management efficiency metric. The experience report of [62] points to metrics related to Lean Thinking and Kanban such as cycle time, number of functionalities in development (working in progress), and system throughput rate, however, both reports do not detail the measurement process, nor how the measurements on the value delivered to customers are applied. Therefore, it is difficult to confirm the effectiveness of the results of the strategies applied to increase customer value, whether positive or negative.

Table 7. Customer value metrics in the context of the ASD.

Theory	Purpose of the measurement	Question to be answered	Metric	Article
VCM	Give flexibility to prioritize the features with higher customer value	What is the level of interdependence of the product features?	- Total dependence for functionality	[42]
	Reduce delivery time for features with higher customer value	How long does it take, on average, to deliver a feature requested by the user until it's available for use?	- Cycle time	[45]
BCM	Manage the customer value of the product under development	How are we delivering customer value?	- Total benefit and cost points, benefit and cost performance index, benefit x cost index, return on investment and productivity of benefit points	[48, 49]
	Increase the performance of delivery of customer value	How effective are we at increasing customer value?	- Productivity of value points, operating expenses by period, amount of work in progress, cycle time, number of critical defects per period, average time to stabilize a release and % of the estimated scope delivered	[14]
MEM	Enhance product customer value	Does the user recognize the value delivered?	- Metrics based on consumer feedback, collected during trials and established by teams according to context. They should describe the behavior of the consumer during the use of the product	[51, 53, 54]

5   Conclusions and Limitations of the Study

As a general answer to the research question that addresses this study: *"How are the strategies currently practiced in the software market to increase CV in the ASD?"*, it was concluded that no study could be found that indicated clearly and deeply what are the strategies to increase customer value in the ASD. Although some studies provide initial contributions as recommendations and results of some strategies, a key implication for research is that further research is still needed, especially through empirical studies. It was found that, with very few exceptions, most of the studies analyzed consider the increase of customer value a high-level perspective. The limitations of the studies analyzed in relation to these strategies implied little or no knowledge about the effective results of their adoptions by the agile teams. Added to this, the lack of customer value measurement methods and metrics prevented any evidence of resulting gains.

It was possible to identify some elements and characteristics that describe the main strategies to maximize customer value in use by the software industry today. The main points identified during this study were organized into three categories: (1) characteristics and strategies of the strategies; (2) approaches, techniques and tools; (3) customer value metrics. However, when compared to the possibilities indicated by the customer value theories in literature, the initiatives are limited and little explored, possibly due to the lack of more empirical knowledge of the key factors for successful deployments and the real impacts they can provide. These issues present themselves as opportunities for future research.

Although the industrial inventory has been conducted from a diverse set of companies, their external validity should be discussed in the interpretation of the study results. Some companies were actively reporting their experiences, while many companies associated with the Agile Alliance did not contribute any reports. The companies that provided the material of the reports of experiences are large companies and represent a specialized knowledge in their sectors. However, the results can still be validated and specified using a larger sample of companies. Despite the above, we were able to discover elements and characteristics of the strategies to increase customer value and to find some evidence of its applications in agile teams.

References

1. Beck, K., et al.: O Manifesto para Desenvolvimento Ágil de Software. http://www.manifestoagil.com.br/
2. Conboy, K.: Agility from first principles: reconstructing the concept of agility in information systems development. Inf. Syst. Res. **20**, 329–354 (2009)
3. Poppendieck, M.: Principles of lean thinking. IT Manag. Sel. **18**, 1–7 (2011)
4. Andreu, L., Sánchez, I., Mele, C.: Value co-creation among retailers and consumers: new insights into the furniture market. J. Retail. Consum. Serv. **17**, 241–250 (2010)
5. Lin, C., Sher, P.J., Shih, H.: Past progress and future directions in conceptualizing customer perceived value. Int. J. Serv. Ind. Manag. **16**, 318–336 (2005)
6. Salleh, C.N., Yahya, Y., Alaa, M., Altemimi, H., Mukhtar, M.: Value co-creation: embedding the value elements in critical success factor for e-government system development. In: 2010 International Symposium on Information Technology, pp. 1–5. IEEE (2010)
7. Racheva, Z., Daneva, M., Sikkel, K., Buglione, L.: Business value is not only dollars – results from case study research on agile software projects. In: Ali Babar, M., Vierimaa, M., Oivo, M. (eds.) PROFES 2010. LNCS, vol. 6156, pp. 131–145. Springer, Heidelberg (2010). https://doi.org/10.1007/978-3-642-13792-1_12

8. Barney, S., Aurum, A., Wohlin, C.: A product management challenge: creating software product value through requirements selection. J. Syst. Archit. **54**, 576–593 (2008)
9. Khalifa, A.S.: Customer value: a review of recent literature and an integrative configuration. Manag. Decis. **42**, 645–666 (2004)
10. Mohammed, I.R., Shankar, R., Banwet, D.K.: Creating flex-lean-agile value chain by outsourcing. Bus. Process Manag. J. **14**, 338–389 (2008)
11. Boehm, B.W.: Value-based software engineering: overview and agenda. In: Biffl, S., Aurum, A., Boehm, B., Erdogmus, H., Grünbacher, P. (eds.) Value-Based Software Engineering, pp. 3–14. Springer, Heidelberg (2006). https://doi.org/10.1007/3-540-29263-2_1
12. Poppendieck, M., Poppendieck, T.: Implementing Lean Software Development: From Concept to Cash. Addison-Wesley, Boston (2007)
13. Johnson, J.: ROI, It's Your Job, Alghero, Itália (2002)
14. Pass, S., Ronen, B.: Reducing the software value gap. Commun. ACM **57**, 80–87 (2014)
15. Forrester: Continuous Delivery: A Maturity Assessment Model. Cambridge, EUA (2013)
16. Alahyari, H., Berntsson Svensson, R., Gorschek, T.: A study of value in agile software development organizations. J. Syst. Softw. **125**, 271–288 (2017)
17. Dingsøyr, T., Nerur, S., Balijepally, V., Moe, N.B.: A decade of agile methodologies: towards explaining agile software development. J. Syst. Softw. **85**, 1213–1221 (2012)
18. Racheva, Z., Daneva, M., Sikkel, K.: Value creation by agile projects: methodology or mystery? In: Bomarius, F., Oivo, M., Jaring, P., Abrahamsson, P. (eds.) PROFES 2009. LNBIP, vol. 32, pp. 141–155. Springer, Heidelberg (2009). https://doi.org/10.1007/978-3-642-02152-7_12
19. Fitzgerald, B., Stol, K.J.: Continuous software engineering: a roadmap and agenda. J. Syst. Softw. **123**, 176–189 (2017)
20. Kitchenham, B., Charters, S.: Guidelines for performing systematic literature reviews in software engineering. Engineering **2**, 1051 (2007)
21. Reichheld, F.F.: Loyalty and the renaissance of marketing. Mark. Manag. **2**, 10–20 (1994)
22. Gilb, T.: Value Planning. Kolbotn, Norway (2017)
23. Kelly, A.: Continuous Digital: An Agile Alternative to Projects. Lean Publishing (2017)
24. Lemon, K.N., Rust, R.T., Zeithaml, V.: What drives customer equity? Mark. Manag. **10**, 20–25 (2001)
25. Kaufman, J.J.: Value Management: Creating Competitive Advantage. Crisp Publications, Menlo Park (1998)
26. Lin, F.-H., et al.: Empirical research on Kano's model and customer satisfaction. PLoS ONE **12**, e0183888 (2017)
27. Huber, F., Herrmann, A., Morgan, R.E.: Gaining competitive advantage through customer value oriented management. J. Consum. Mark. **18**, 41–53 (2001)
28. Thiry, M.: A Framework for Value Management Practice. Project Management Institute (2013)
29. de Chernatony, L., Harris, F., Dall'Olmo, F.R.: Added value: its nature roles and sustainability. Eur. J. Mark. **34**, 39–56 (2001)
30. Lin, P.-C., Huang, Y.-H.: The influence factors on choice behavior regarding green products based on the theory of consumption values. J. Clean. Prod. **22**, 11–18 (2012)
31. Fenwick, N., Matzke, P., Shey, H., Wang, C., Klehm, R., McPherson, I.: The 2016 Guide to Digital Predators, Transformers, and Dinosaurs (2016). https://www.forrester.com/report/The+2016+Guide+To+Digital+Predators+Transformers+And+Dinosaurs/
32. Lanning, M.J.: Delivering Profitable Value: A Revolutionary Framework to Accelerate Growth, Generate Wealth, and Rediscover the Heart of Business. Perseus Books, New York (1998)

33. Verhoef, P.C., Lemon, K.N., Parasuraman, A., Roggeveen, A., Tsiros, M., Schlesinger, L. A.: Customer experience creation: determinants, dynamics and management strategies. J. Retail. **85**, 31–41 (2009)
34. Covin, J.G., Garrett, R.P., Kuratko, D.F., Shepherd, D.A.: Value proposition evolution and the performance of internal corporate ventures. J. Bus. Ventur. **30**, 749–774 (2015)
35. Vargo, S.L., Maglio, P.P., Akaka, M.A.: On value and value co-creation: a service systems and service logic perspective. Eur. Manag. J. **26**, 145–152 (2008)
36. McKean, J.: Customers are People: The Human Touch. Wiley, Chichester (2002)
37. Gentile, C., Spiller, N., Noci, G.: How to sustain the customer experience. Eur. Manag. J. **25**, 395–410 (2007)
38. Schneider, B., Bowen, D.E.: Understanding customer delight and outrage. Sloan Manag. Rev. **41**, 35–45 (1999)
39. Kaikkonen, H., Härkönen, J., Haapasalo, H., Rodríguez, P.: Supporting lean software enterprises with agile development methods identifying the relationship between lean and agile. Parallel Cloud Comput. Res. **2**, 1–12 (2014)
40. Larman, C., Vodde, B.: Scaling Lean & Agile Development: Thinking and Organizational Tools for Large-Scale Scrum. Addison-Wesley Professional, Boston (2008)
41. Anand, R.V., Dinakaran, M.: Handling stakeholder conflict by agile requirement prioritization using Apriori technique. Comput. Electr. Eng. **61**, 126–136 (2017)
42. Scheerer, A., Bick, S., Hildenbrand, T., Heinzl, A.: The effects of team backlog dependencies on agile multiteam systems: a graph theoretical approach. In: 2015 48th Hawaii International Conference on System Sciences, pp. 5124–5132. IEEE (2015)
43. Daneva, M., et al.: Agile requirements prioritization in large-scale outsourced system projects: an empirical study. J. Syst. Softw. **86**, 1333–1353 (2013)
44. Komssi, M., Kauppinen, M., Töhönen, H., Lehtola, L., Davis, A.M.: Roadmapping problems in practice: value creation from the perspective of the customers. Requir. Eng. **20**, 45–69 (2015)
45. Vlietland, J., van Solingen, R., van Vliet, H.: Aligning codependent Scrum teams to enable fast business value delivery: a governance framework and set of intervention actions. J. Syst. Softw. **113**, 418–429 (2016)
46. Staron, M., Meding, W.: MetricsCloud: scaling-up metrics dissemination in large organizations. Adv. Softw. Eng. **2014**, 1–12 (2014)
47. Cedergren, S., Larsson, S.: Evaluating performance in the development of software-intensive products. Inf. Softw. Technol. **56**, 516–526 (2014)
48. Hannay, J.E., Benestad, H.C., Strand, K.: Earned business value: see that you deliver value to your customer. IEEE Softw. **34**, 58–70 (2017)
49. Torrecilla-Salinas, C.J., Sedeño, J., Escalona, M.J., Mejías, M.: Estimating, planning and managing Agile Web development projects under a value-based perspective. Inf. Softw. Technol. **61**, 124–144 (2015)
50. Tuan, N.N., Thang, H.Q.: Combining maturity with agility. In: Proceedings of the Fourth Symposium on Information and Communication Technology - SoICT 2013, pp. 267–274. ACM Press, New York (2013)
51. Ehrenhard, M., Wijnhoven, F., van den Broek, T., Zinck Stagno, M.: Unlocking how start-ups create business value with mobile applications: development of an App-enabled Business Innovation Cycle. Technol. Forecast. Soc. Change **115**, 26–36 (2017)
52. Fagerholm, F., Sanchez Guinea, A., Mäenpää, H., Münch, J.: The RIGHT model for continuous experimentation. J. Syst. Softw. **123**, 292–305 (2017)
53. Vidgen, R., Shaw, S., Grant, D.B.: Management challenges in creating value from business analytics. Eur. J. Oper. Res. **261**, 626–639 (2017)

54. Lindgren, E., Münch, J.: Raising the odds of success: the current state of experimentation in product development. Inf. Softw. Technol. **77**, 80–91 (2016)
55. Khurum, M., Gorschek, T., Wilson, M.: The software value map - an exhaustive collection of value aspects for the development of software intensive products. J. Softw. Evol. Process. **25**, 711–741 (2013)
56. Man, Y., Oren, I.: Developing Avionic Products Using Lean-Agile at Elbit Systems (2017)
57. Koski, A., Mikkonen, T.: Taming a Monster: Tackling the Emergent Issues Encountered in Mission Critical System Development (2017)
58. Edwards, K.: Partnering to Improve Usability (2017)
59. Wang, X., Khanna, D., Mondini, M., Pantiuchina, J., Stillittano, G.: Experiment with MVPs: The First "Startuppuccino" Steps to a Lean Edtech Startup (2017)
60. Helfand, H.: Dynamic Reteaming: How We Thrive by Rebuilding Teams (2016)
61. Silva, J.: Lean Sales Up – Making value from product conception (2015)
62. Singh, P., Vacanti, D.S.: Ultimate Kanban: Scaling Agile Without Frameworks at Ultimate Software (2016)
63. Barrett, S.: The Final Frontier Aligning the enterprise's direction and your crew's efforts (2017)

Towards an Agile Development Environment

Marcelo Lessa Ribeiro[✉] and Itana Maria de Souza Gimenes

Departamento de Informática, Universidade Estadual de Maringá,
Maringá, PR, Brazil
mlessaribeiro@gmail.com, itana@gmail.com
http://din.uem.br

Abstract. The demand for software engineering support environment
was evident since the 70s. It was necessary to control the integration
between processes, tools and developers in order to increase software
quality and productivity. Research projects produced several environments which introduced important concepts such as central artefact
repository, well-defined and enactable software processes, as well as supporting tools. Later, agile methods emerged as a solution to overcome
strict software processes, however it also demanded support tools to facilitate its adoption in software organizations. Several works report the use
of agile practices and support tools, however, they do not bring about
the structure of a software engineering environment that integrates the
managerial cycle and agile practices. This paper presents the design of
a software engineering environment which is based on Application Life
Cycle (ALM) and SCRUM principles integrated with management and
construction tools. The proposed design was validated with practitioners and a comparison with previous development environment is also
presented. This work contributes to support novel enterprises to set up
a work environment for agile practices.

Keywords: Agile methods · Agile practices ·
Software engineering environment

1 Introduction

The demand for software engineering support environment was evident since
the 70s [1]. It was necessary to control the integration between processes, tools
and developers in order to increase software quality and productivity. Research
projects produced several environments which introduced important concepts
such as central artefact repository, well-defined and enactable software processes,
as well as supporting tools such as configuration and version management [2].

Another important concept in this context was Application Life Cycle Management (ALM). It is a model that covers software activities from conception to
maintenance [3]. ALM brings about concepts to support the articulation between
managerial tasks and the technical development operations [4] in a similar way

© Springer Nature Switzerland AG 2019
G. S. Tonin et al. (Eds.): WBMA 2018, CCIS 981, pp. 80–94, 2019.
https://doi.org/10.1007/978-3-030-14310-7_6

to software process but more flexible. ALM help us to think on how the research developed in the software engineering environment context can be applied to support agile methods.

Agile methods emerged as a solution to overcome strict software processes, however it also demanded support environment to facilitate its adoption in software organizations [5,6]. Agile methods need supporting tools to control its inherent nature of constantly evolve and test software as well the cooperation between developers and customers throughout the software life cycle [4].

Software industry had to look for new managerial approaches and tools which also included the reuse of previous concepts developed within software engineering environments. Thus, the design of a support environment for agile methods requires a research that takes into account the experiences of both industry and academic research [4]. The evidences provided by industry are extremely relevant in the context of agile methods [7].

Several works report the use of agile practices and supporting tools, however, they do not bring about the structure of a supporting software engineering environment that integrates a managerial cycle such as ALM and agile practices [8–11].

This paper presents the design of a software engineering environment, named Agile Development Environment (ADE), which is based on ALM and SCRUM principles integrated with management and construction tools. SCRUM is used because it has been considered technically efficient and it has been widely used in industry [12,13]. ALM principles were adopted because it offers flexible concepts that join governance, development and maintenance of software [14,15].

The organization of this paper is as follows: Sect. 2 presents the background for the research developed; Sect. 3 presents the specification of the proposed environment, named Agile Development Environment (ADE); Sect. 4 presents the ADE evatuation; and, Sect. 5 presents the conclusions.

2   Background

The work presented in this paper is supported by the research developed in three main areas: agile methods, software engineering environments and ALM. The principles originated from these areas together with the current state of agile practices in software industry form the basis of ADE design.

Agile methods represent a breakthrough in software development as it opposes to traditional methods and have been progressively adopted by software industry. These methods admit that software changes are part of the software process instead of eliminating them based on planning and a rigorous process [16]. They believe in the client satisfaction through the delivery of small and frequent versions of products.

Several agile methods have been developed such as SCRUM, Extreme Programming, Crystal and FDD. SCRUM [17] has been pointed out as one of the most popular method in industry [13]. Its main focus is on agile project management in iterative cycles that can be flexibly combined with software development techniques. Therefore, we selected SCRUM as the basis for the ADE software process.

The most used practices in the context of agile methods selected to design ADE were based on Extreme Programming and the investigations of [9,13,18]. The practices are: Test Driven Development (TDD); Continuous Integration; Continuous Delivery; Refactoring; Code Revision; Code Quality Analysis; and, User's stories.

Our challenge is to reflect on the research work carried in context of Software Engineering Environments (SEE) and Process-centred Software Engineering Environment (PSEE) in order to propose the design of a support environment to fulfil the basic needs of agile methods mainly focusing on small companies that face the need to define low cost supporting tools to develop their projects.

The need for well-defined processes and tools to support software development is recognized since the 70s [1]. This led to the proposal of several SEE [19]. One of the key issues in SEE is how to provide tool integration [20]. A common approach to this issue is to view integration in four dimensions [20,21] as follows: (i) Data integration; (ii) control integration; (iii) process integration; and, presentation. The environments which provide support for automated process definition and execution are named PSEE [2,22–24].

Software industry faced difficult to adopt SEE and PSEE due to the common agreement needed to reach standards like PCTE. In addition, it was difficult to find universal software process programming language and process enactment machines.

ALM is a similar concept to software process as in PSEE [14,15]. It is based on a cycle that involves governance, development and maintenance [25]. However, ALM focus on the development cycle: requirement, design, coding, test and project management [26].

Thus, ADE adopts the concept of ALM because it is more flexible and compatible with agile methods than the rigorous process automation conceived in PSEE.

3   ADE

The ADE design is based on the following principles: (i) SCRUM as a method for project management; (ii) ALM as the development cycle; (iii) the dimensions of tool integration defined in [21] which consists of process, data and control.

SCRUM was adopted because it is the most used management method in industry software [13]. It has been reported that this method facilitates activity control, resource optimization and realistic estimations [12].

ALM brings about principles of life cycle management that includes governance, development and maintenance [14,15]. ALM also promotes project management based on agile methods [6].

Tool integration aims to promote the systematic use of tools and agile practices which are essential to automate the development process [27]. The dimensions of tool integration considered are: data, control and process [21,28]. The data dimension will support the exchange of artefact between tools; the control dimension articulates the sequence of tool invocation when possible; and, the process will guide the SCRUM managerial activities as well as the technical tasks.

3.1   ADE Architecture

The main practices selected to compose ADE correspond to functionalities consistently applied in agile development. They are: project management; versioning control; code revision; continuous integration; and, code quality analysis. Each of these practices constitutes an element of the ADE architecture to which there is a correspondent support tool.

The logical architecture of ADE, as presented in Fig. 1, shows the relationship between its elements. This architecture was designed to integrate the Project Management support with tools that automate the main practices of the environment. These practices are described as follows.

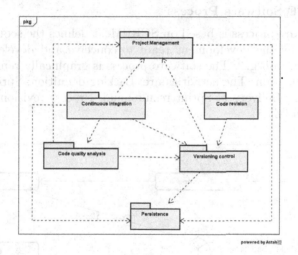

Fig. 1. Overview of ADE architecture

Project Management: responsible for the management of the development activities. It supports the definition of the overall development process. In the case of ADE the high level activities are based on SCRUM from which smaller tasks are created. ADE functionalities include: effort estimate; task time recording; functionality priorization.

Versioning Control: it is responsible for the source code versioning, the tracing of updates and version recovery. The code is traced based on the commits carried out by the version control tool.

Code Revision: responsible for supporting the revision of code for the identification of eventual errors or improvements required [29].

Continuous Integration: it does the continuous integration of code produced by the developers so that overall code is continuous generated. Each code integration interacts with the compiler to build a new system version. In addition, it triggers the automated testing tools to detect errors [30].

Code Quality Analysis: responsible for monitoring the quality of the source code to produce metrics such as: coupling, cohesion, duplicated code, technical debt, test coverage and development patterns. The analysis of these metrics support decision making.

Persintence: it facilitates the artefact persistence. It is represented as one element; however, each correspondent tool has its own storing mechanism that can be a database or the file system. Thus ADE does not adopt a common database; when necessary data are exchanged is carried out at the file system level using XML.

3.2   The ADE Software Process

The ADE software process is based on SCRUM. It defines the sequence of steps to be followed by the development team to conceive and develop a software system as shown in Fig. 2. The software process is graphically represented by a UML activity diagram. The activities are: Backlog definition; Sprint definition; Sprint execution; Delivery of Sprint results; and, Process revision. These steps are described as follows.

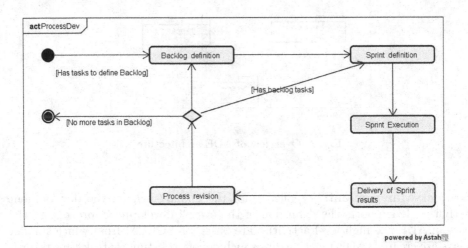

Fig. 2. ADE software process

Step 1 – Backlog definition - it is divided into 3 tasks: analysis, Backlog creation and Backlog priorization. The analysis aims to understand the target software so that the Product Owner (PO) can have a vision of its requirements. These requirements are expressed as users' stories where each story represents a functionality. These stories are represented as a task in the project management supporting tool. The task can be divided into smaller ones. The Backlog is composed of the defined stories. At the end, the stories are prioritized and the sequence of the tasks execution is defined.

Step 2 – Sprint definition - this step undertakes a Sprint planning meeting in which the PO, the SRUM master and the development team select the tasks, defined the project management tool, to compose the Sprint backlog. These tasks are then estimated based on the Planning Poker Technique. Each task is updated registering its estimation. In addition, the development team defines how the task will be implemented and the team member associated with it. The Sprint backlog establish the functionalities which is to be delivered by the sprint.

Step 3 – Sprint Execution - this step executes the Sprint Backlog. The control of the Sprint Backlog is undertaken through daily meetings between the SCRUM master and the development team in order to identify. Finally, the identification and analysis of problems that might occur with the Sprint delivery is carried out.

To implement each task of the Backlog five steps are executed as represented in Fig. 3: implementation, automated testing, manual testing, code revision and integration. These steps are summarized as follows.

– **Implementation**: the respective story is codified according to the decision taken in Step 2.
– **Automated testing**: it undertakes the automated testing of the code generated. An iteration between these steps must occur to increase the test coverage thus increasing software quality and reducing defects [31,32].
– **Manual testing**: in this step manual tests of the implemented functionality are undertaken to ensure the quality of the software. The code revision tool can support the identification of the parts of the code impacted by the error detection.
– **Code revision**: every code developed must be revised by a team member different from the one who developed it in order to increase the chances of identify errors. The project management tool helps to guarantee the correct participant assignment. This tool also helps to highlight the updated code.
– **Continuous integration**: the produced code must be integrated with the existing ones to generate a new software baseline. This step is undertaken automatically. In addition, the integrator will dispatch the analysis of code quality which includes out the test coverage analysis, duplication quantity, software complexity, amount of comments, technical debt, amount of comments and code patterns. The result of the analysis must be available for the development team.When the quality rules fail the integrator automatically creates a task in the project manager.

Step 4 – Delivery of Sprint results – at the Sprint end a new version of the software containing the new functionalities is generated. This is undertaken by the integration team.

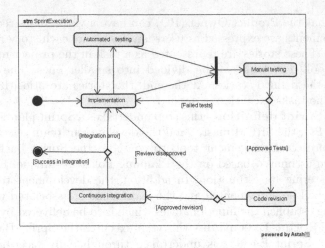

Fig. 3. Sprint execution

Step 5 – Process revision – the last step of the process is the Sprint retrospective. It supports the PO, the SCRUM master and the development team to revise eventual problems that still remains in the Sprint execution, such as problems with communication with client, requirement misunderstanding, bad task estimation and increase of technical debt. Thus, this step supports an inspection that can lead to process adaptation that might improve the next Sprint. At the end of Step5, if there are tasks to be carried out in the project management tool, another Sprint cycle is started.

3.3   An Example of ADE Instantiation

ADE design has presented the main conceptual elements of its architecture. However, it has to be instantiated with tools, according to the organization resources and culture. This section presents an ADE instantiation populated with free software tools.

The tools were selected based on the agile methods literature review, such as SonarQube [33], Gerrit [34] and Redmine [13]. The relationship between these tools is shown in Fig. 4.

Table 1 presents the elements and the correspondent tool adopted to instantiate ADE.

4   ADE Evaluation

The ADE evaluation is composed of two parts. The first is a comparison between ADE and main aspects proposed in previous PSEE. The second part is an empirical qualitative study which aims to provide preliminary evidences of ADE feasibility.

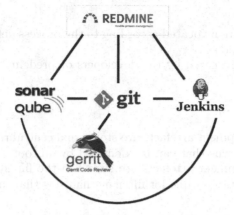

Fig. 4. Example of ADE instantiation

Table 1. ADE elements and correspondent tools

Elements	Tools
Project management	Redmine
Versioning control	Git
Code revision	Gerrit
Continuous integration	Jenkins
Code quality analysis	Sonar qube

4.1   Comparison Between ADE and PSEE

The parameters selected to compare ADE to PSEE proposed in the literature are: process definition; team management; tool integration; data integration; configuration and version management; and, evolvability. As a result, are presents the similarities and differences analyzed.

Process Definition and Evolution

- **PSSE** Proposes a Process Modelling language (PML) to specify the process and an engine to execute it.
- **ADE** Adopts the Scrum process and uses a Project management tool where the activities are specified but do not control the process execution. The maintenance of the activities is controlled by the project manager.

Team Management

- **PSSE** Team allocation is specified in the software process.
- **ADE** Team allocation is specified in the project management tool according to the SCRUM responsibilities.

Tool Integration

- **PSSE** The tools are invocated according to the process definition throughout the process execution.
- **ADE** Tools are invocated by the developers or predefined scripts according to the tool kit used.

Data Integration

- **PSSE** The development artefacts are stored in a central repository according to predefined patterns that can be identified by all tools.
- **ADE** The development artefacts are stored in the file system or databases and the tools are responsible for filter mechanisms that might be necessary.

Configuration and Version Management

- **PSSE** Adopt configuration and version management mechanism proper of the environment as a horizontal tool.
- **ADE** Uses configuration and version management tools well known in the market and do not suppose internal mechanisms.

Evolvability

- **PSSE** The capacity of evolution depends on the conformity of the tools to the process and central repository patterns.
- **ADE** There is flexibility of tool aggregation because it is based on the file level or databases and tool invocation.

The information provided in this sub section reveals that a strict process specification and an automated process execution were not adopted within the agile context. The tool market has been driven by flexibility and tool independence. Data are exchanged at the file level using XML format and filters. In addition, project management tools have become increasingly important and are the main mechanism for registering the process activities. The emphasis of the technical tools has been on the implementation, test and code analysis due to the agile method principles. Concepts like configuration and version management developed within the SEE research context have become a standard.

4.2   Qualitative Empirical Study

This study is based on concepts of Grounded Theory such as Coding as proposed by [35] that complements the sequential strategy of mixed-methods according to [36–38]. The relevant concepts of the study are represented through codes identified in the specialist answers.

Coding is part of the procedures to provide basis for conceptualization, reducing data and elaborating categories according to data properties and dimensions [39]. In this study it was used Open Coding and Axial Coding [35].

The main objective of the study is to analyze the ADE design as a feasible mechanism to support the development of software based on agile methods.

Result Analysis. The study sample consists of seven specialists selected based on their experience in industry developing projects with agile methods. The participants involved 7 software practioners working in industry distributed, according to their graduation level, as follows: one master student (14.3%), 5 with specialization degree (71.4%); and one doing specialization (14.3%).

An electronic form composed of seven questions was elaborated. Each participant received an email with the form access information and the study instrumentalization.

The tool used to organize and codify the data collected from specialist was Dedoose. The procedure used was open coding. Next, codes were categorized based on axial coding and graphically represented. Three code categories emerged: Utilization provides benefits; possible improvements and difficulties of adoption. Figure 5 presents the Category Utilization provides benefits and their refinements which indicate that, according to the participants ADE: Contributes to productivity; Supports project management; Increases the chances of obtaining quality software; Process is complete and Tool integration is effective.

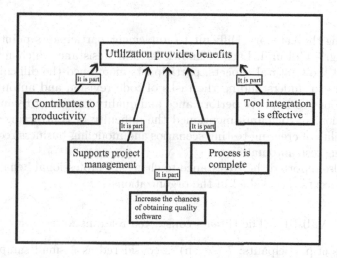

Fig. 5. Graphical representation of codes related to the Category Utilization provides benefits

Regarding to Possible Improvements, as shown in Fig. 6, the participants mainly pointed out that ADE could include New tools, such as tools to trace requirements and support deployment. Second, it was suggested that ADE should provide mechanisms for Learning with the Sprint results, thus supporting continuous learning.

The category Process is complete includes codes such as include tasks to support pair programming and move people around to support crossed training between areas of knowledge.

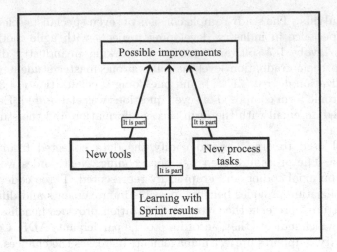

Fig. 6. Graphical representation of codes related to the Category Possible improvements

Regarding the category Difficult to implement participants pointed out, as shown in Fig. 7: Cultural, Lack of knowledge and Resistance to change.

Amongst the Cultural aspects, participants mentioned the difficulties of the organizations to understanding the tasks of code revision and automated tests as contributions to improve performance and quality instead of resource waste.

In addition, participants mentioned the difficulty of contracting specialists with the ability of creating testing scenarios and modeling business requirements to facilitating test automation.

It was also reported the Resistance to change of professional behavior due to previous concepts established in the organizations.

Threats to Validity. The threats considered relevant were:

- Numbers of participants: 7 (seven) is considered as a small sample. This is compensated by the knowledge of specialist.
- The level of knowledge required in the development of agile projects and tools of the subjects was considered satisfactory for the technical analysis; however a construct threat is the lack of tests to validate the questionnaire understanding of the participants.
- Training was undertaken to reduce the stress effects on participants. Instrumentations were also sent by mail to them.
- The objective of the study was to work with post-graduated professional with practical experience in the development of agile projects and development tools. However, this turn out to be impossible. Thus, only a small sample was possible.

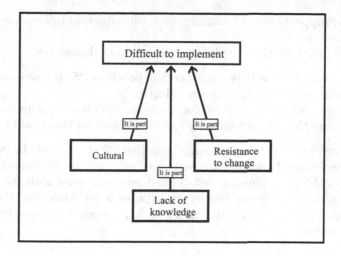

Fig. 7. Graphical representation of codes related to the Category Difficult to implement

Discussion. The analysis and interpretation of the study results led to three categories and respective codes to summarize the evaluation of ADE feasibility. In addition, the results contribute to identify limitations and propose improvements.

The specialist stated ADE provides resources to support a manageable process that can lead to the improvement of the software quality. Tool integration is effective and can support the continuous evolution of the software.

5 Conclusions

This research presents the design of a software engineering environment within the context of agile methods, named ADE.

The introduction of agile methods also need tools and support environment to develop software in a manageable environment [6]. Previous development environments were based on a strict software process that does not fit with the flexibility of agile methods.

ADE is based on SCRUM as a management method for agile development due its indication from the literature review and its dissemination in industry [12,13]. The practices selected to compose ADE were mainly based on [13] and [9]. In addition, ADE apply principles of ALM to articulate SCRUM with development practices because its concepts offer support to manage the software life cycle taking into account governance, development and maintenance [14,15].

The research developed contributes to show how is the articulation of the software process and agile practices, techniques and tools as well as showing how previous research on PSEE influenced the current environment in industry.

The empirical qualitative study carried out indicates that ADE is feasible and brings benefits to developers such as: promotes software quality; improves productivity; supports project management; supports tool integration and facilitates evolvability.

Additional contributions of the research on ADE design are:

- Presents a comparison between aspects of previous PSEE research and what has actually been used in software industry.
- Constitutes a reference to small companies to set up a development environment because they do not have resources to invest on this kind of research.

Finally, we observed that it is surprising that 30 years after the emblematic statement "Software Processes are Software too" [40], organizations still have difficult to establish a minimal well-defined processe, even with the flexibility of agile methods and the availability of software tools. Moreover, there is still a lack of specialized professional abilities such as requirement specification and testing automation.

References

1. Brown, A.W.: An examination of the current state of ipse technology. In: Proceedings of 15th International Conference on Software Engineering, pp. 338–347 (1993)
2. Finkelstein, A., Kramer, J., Nuseibech, B.: Software Process Modelling and Technology. Wiley, New York (1994)
3. Lacheiner, H., Ramler, R.: Application lifecycle management as infrastructure for software process improvement and evolution: experience and insights from industry. In: 37th EUROMICRO Conference on Software Engineering and Advanced Applications, pp. 286–293 (2011)
4. Fuggetta, A., Di Nitto, E.: Software process. In: Proceedings of the on Future of Software Engineering, pp. 1–12. ACM, New York (2014)
5. Beck, K.: Extreme Programming Explained: Embrace Change, 2nd edn. Addison-Wesley, Boston (2004)
6. Franky, M.C.: Agile management and development of software projects based on collaborative environments. In: SIGSOFT Software Engineering, pp. 1–6 (2011)
7. Gregory, P., Barroca, L., Taylor, K., Salah, D., Sharp, H.: Agile challenges in practice: a thematic analysis. In: Lassenius, C., Dingsøyr, T., Paasivaara, M. (eds.) XP 2015. LNBIP, vol. 212, pp. 64–80. Springer, Cham (2015). https://doi.org/10.1007/978-3-319-18612-2_6
8. Humble, J., Farley, D.: Continuous Delivery: Reliable Software Releases Through Build, Test, and Deployment Automation. Addison-Wesley, Boston (2010)
9. Abrantes, J.F., Travassos, G.H.: Common agile practices in software processes. In: International Symposium on Empirical Software Engineering and Measurement, pp. 355–358 (2011)
10. Bass, J.M.: Influences on agile practice tailoring in enterprise software development. In: Agile India, pp. 1–9 (2012)
11. Collins, E., Dias-Neto, A., de Lucena Jr., V.F.: Strategies for agile software testing automation: an industrial experience. In: IEEE 36th Annual Computer Software and Applications Conference Workshops, pp. 440–445 (2012)
12. Striebeck, M.: Ssh! we are adding a process... [agile practices]. In: AGILE 2006, pp. 185–193 (2006)

13. VersionOne 10th annual state of agile survery (2015). http://www.versionone.com
14. Chappel, D.: What is application lifecyle management? Technical report, David Chappel & Associates (2014). http://www.davidchappell.com/writing/white_papers/What-is-ALM-Chappell.pdf
15. Rossman, B.: Application Lifecycle Management Activities, Methodologies, Disciplines, Tools, Benefits, ALM Tools and Products. Emereo Pty Ltd, London (2010)
16. Highsmith, J., Cockburn, A.: Agile software development: the business of innovation. In: Computer, pp. 120–122 (2001)
17. Schwaber K., Sutherland J.: Scrum guide (2013). http://www.scrumguides.org/docs/scrumguide/v1/Scrum-Guide-Portuguese-BR.pdf
18. Melo, C.O., Santos, V.A., Corbucci, H., Katayama, E., Goldman, A., Kon, F.: Métodos Ágeis no brasil: Estado da prática em times e organizações (2012). http://ccsl.ime.usp.br/agilcoop/artigos
19. Oinas-Kukkonen, H., Rossi, G.: On two approaches to software repositories and hypertext functionality. J. Digit. Inf. (1999). https://journals.tdl.org/jodi/index.php/jodi/article/view/14/13
20. Wasserman, A.I.: Tool integration in software engineering environments. In: Proceedings of the International Workshop on Environments on Software Engineering Environments, pp. 137–149 (1990)
21. Thomas, I., Nejmeh, B.A.: Definitions of tool integration for environments. IEEE Softw. **9**, 29–35 (1992)
22. Gimenes, I.M.S., Weiss, G.M., Huzita, E.H.M.: Um Padrão para Definição de um Gerenciador de Processos de Software. In: Jornadas Iberoamericanas de Ingenieria de Requisitos y Ambientes de Software, Alajuela, Costa Rica (1999)
23. Bandinelli, S., Nitto, E.D., Fuggetta, A.: Supporting cooperation in the SPADE-1 environment. IEEE Trans. Softw. Eng. 841–865 (1996)
24. Fuggetta, A.: Functionality and architecture of PSEE. Inf. Softw. Technol. **38**, 289–293 (1996)
25. Baessa, H.J.O.: Gestão do ciclo de vida das aplicações: análise do sap solution manager. Master's thesis, Instituto Superior de Estatística e Gestão de Informação Universidade Nova de Lisboa (2011)
26. Kovair, M.: ALM and Integrated ALM (2016). http://www.kovair.com/What-are-ALM-and-Integrated-ALM.pdf
27. Kravchik, M.: Application lifecycle management environments: past, present and future. Master's thesis, The Open University of Israel (2009)
28. Betemps, C.M.: Ambientes de desenvolvimento de software baseados em workflow. Master's thesis, Universidade Federal do Rio Grande do Sul (2003)
29. Sommerville, I.: Software Engineering. Addison-Wesley, Boston (2010)
30. Fowler, M.: Continuous integration (2006). http://martinfowler.com/articles/continuousIntegration.html
31. Maximilien, E.M., Williams, L.: Assessing test-driven development at IBM. In: 25th International Conference on Software Engineering, pp. 564–569 (2003)
32. George, B., Williams, L.: A structured experiment of test-driven development. Inf. Softw. Technol. **46**, 337–342 (2004)
33. Ferenc, R., Lang, L., Siket, I., Gyimthy, T., Bakota, T.: Source meter sonar qube plug-in. In: IEEE 14th International Working Conference on Source Code Analysis and Manipulation, pp. 77–82 (2014)
34. Rigby, P., Cleary, B., Painchaud, F., Storey, M.A., German, D.: Contemporary peer review in action: lessons from open source development. IEEE Softw. **29**, 56–61 (2012)

35. Corbin, J.M., Strauss, A.: Basics of Qualitative Research: Techniques and Procedures for Developing Grounded Theory, 3rd edn. Sage Publications, Beverley Hills (2008)
36. Seaman, C.B.: Qualitative methods in empirical studies of software engineering. IEEE Trans. Softw. Eng. 557–572 (1999)
37. Dyba, T., Prikladnicki, R., Rönkkö, K., Seaman, C., Sillito, J.: Qualitative research in software engineering. Empirical Softw. Eng. **16**, 425–429 (2011)
38. Creswell, J.W., Clark, V.L.P.: Designing and Conducting Mixed Methods Research, 2nd edn. Sage Publications, Beverley Hills (2010)
39. Broberg, L.L.: A grounded theory approach to examining design and usability guidelines for four-year tribal college web sites. Ph.D. thesis (2011)
40. Osterweil, L.: Software processes are software too. In: Proceedings of the 9th International Conference on Software Engineering, pp. 2–13 (1987)

Short Paper

Scrum in a Strongly Hierarchical Organization

Fernando Rodrigues de Sá(✉), Everton Luiz de Resende Lucas,
and Adelmo Dias de Oliveira

Centro de Computação da Aeronáutica de São José dos Campos,
Praça Marechal do Ar Eduardo Gomes, n° 50 - Vila das Acácias,
São José dos Campos, SP 12228-901, Brazil
{desafrs,evertonelrl,adelmoado}@fab.mil.br

Abstract. One of the duties of the Aeronautics Computing Center of
São José dos Campos, Organization of the Brazilian Air Force, is to
develop and operate Information Technology projects and applications
assigned to it. As a Military Organization, this Center is constitution-
ally organized based on hierarchy and discipline. For the management
of their projects, the software developers of this Military Organization
decided to use Scrum and its good practices. However, the use of an agile
framework implies in the horizontal interaction between the members of
a team, without any hierarchy between them. At first, the use of Agile
Methods in the military was opposed to the hierarchy, reflecting in the
relationship between people and the quality of the product. This work
aims to present the resources used for a healthy application of Agile
Methods in an environment strongly based on the hierarchy between
people, improving not only the relationship between them, but also the
quality of the products they develop.

Keywords: Agile Methods · Scrum ·
Hierarchical organizational structure

1 Introduction

Constituted by the Navy, the Army and the Air Force, the Brazilian Armed
Forces are permanent and regular national institutions, under the supreme
authority of the President of the Republic, and are destined to the defense of the
Motherland, to the guarantee of the constitutional powers and, at the initiative
of any of these, of law and order [1].

By normative force of the Constitution, these institutions are organized on
the basis of hierarchy and discipline. Their members form a special category of
servants of the Homeland and are called military.

The military hierarchy is the ordering of authority, at different levels, within
the structure of the Armed Forces. The ordination is done by posts or gradu-
ations; within the same post or graduation is done by seniority at the post or

© Springer Nature Switzerland AG 2019
G. S. Tonin et al. (Eds.): WBMA 2018, CCIS 981, pp. 97–102, 2019.
https://doi.org/10.1007/978-3-030-14310-7_7

graduation. Respect for the hierarchy is embodied in the spirit of compliance with the sequence of authority [2].

Within the scope of the Brazilian Air Force, the Aeronautics Computing Centers (CCA), organizations foreseen by Decree No. 7,069, of January 20, 2010, have the purpose of managing the Information Technology systems and services under their responsibility [3].

The Aeronautics Computing Center of São José dos Campos (CCA-SJ), which originated from the former Nucleus of the Data Processing Center (NCPD) of the Brazilian Aeronautics Institute of Technology (ITA), among its attributions and competencies, operates as an agency for IT systems and projects. To this end, the CCA-SJ has in its military personnel the most diverse areas of training related to IT careers, such as computer engineers, systems analysts, computer technicians, among others.

Projects and systems developed by this CCA are aimed at various purposes, including:

- archival and document management;
- command and control;
- visual scenarios for flight simulators;
- low cost flight simulators;
- among others.

To manage the development of its portfolio, the CCA-SJ adopts agile methodologies, such as Scrum. But in Scrum, the Development Teams are self-organized, meaning no one tells you how the work should be done. These teams are structured and authorized to organize their own work. In addition, Scrum does not recognize titles for members of its development teams. Therefore, there is no hierarchy among the members of Scrum Teams [5].

CCA-SJ Development Teams are composed by military personnel, with strong hierarchical links between them. They make part of Sections, which are organized based on their assignments, such as software testing or database, for example. In a Military Organization, these Sections are also organized hierarchically, within their organizational structure.

With this, a strong contradiction between the characteristics of the Scrum and the militarism is perceived. While members of Scrum Teams are organized horizontally, with no hierarchy between them, the military are organized into an essentially vertical structure, with a strongly present hierarchy.

The use of Scrum in the CCA-SJ environment, even being an initiative from members of Development Teams themselves, presents some conflicts that will be discussed throughout this article. Based on these conflicts, militaries from CCA-SJ are undertaking a work of change in their organizational culture to improve the performance of the Teams.

In this way, the objective of this article is to present a story of experience about Scrum in the CCA-SJ. This is a work in progress in order to adapt its use within this Military Organization of the Brazilian Air Force.

Section 2 presents Problem Identification about the use of Scrum in the CCA-SJ, the Problem Handling, the Action Plan, the Problem Solving and Trainings for Development Teams. Section 3 presents the first results, once this is a work in progress. Section 4 presents some final considerations about this article.

2   Scrum in the CCA-SJ

As mentioned in the previous section, the use of Scrum in the CCA-SJ started as an initiative of militaries themselves working at development of projects and systems.

For the adoption of Scrum, no training was carried out. Some military had previous knowledge of the framework, learned at academic or business institutions. With this, at the beginning of its adoption, the Scrum was applied in a partial way, not contemplating all of its artifacts and ceremonies [4].

2.1   Problem Identification

In the middle of 2017, communication problems were identified between the Development Team of one of the systems under the responsibility of the CCA-SJ and the Section responsible for customer services.

With that, it was decided to include members from this Section in the Daily Meetings, in order to solve this problem. In addition, specific works have been done to identify the most significant aspects that have influenced communication problems in order to mitigate them.

However, in the first quarter of 2018, a number of problems were identified in this system, which resulted in delivery delays and malfunctioning.

2.2   Problem Handling

In the second quarter of 2018, it was decided to reorganize the development team. From that moment, positive changes began to happen.

An Internal Commission for Implementation of a Project Management Office (PMO) at the CCA-SJ was created in order to standardize project-related governance processes and facilitate the sharing of resources, methodologies, tools and techniques.

This Committee is composed of 3 ranked officers, one sublieutenant and one civilian servant, with diverse knowledge in the area of IT and processes. PMO was given the task of standardizing, monitoring and advising on the implementation of CCA-SJ projects.

The first action of the PMO was to conduct an Organizational Climate Survey with those military directly involved in the development of systems. This research pointed to several factors that contribute to the low level of satisfaction of these military, which influence productivity and quality of the products delivered to the customers. Among those factors, the ones that most attracted the attention of the PMO were:

– hierarchical decisions were made instead of technical decisions;

- several military was not worth for their work;
- low level of satisfaction in relationship with superiors;
- communication problems; and
- lack of support from the chain of command.

2.3   Action Plan

After the survey results analysis, an Action Plan was drawn up in order to mitigate the problems presented and allow the use of Scrum within this strongly hierarchical environment. To allow Teams technical decisions, the following objectives were defined:

- perform group dynamics; and
- guide Product Owners and Scrum Masters not to allow hierarchical decisions.

In order to better value military for their works, the following objectives were defined:

- create a Career Plan for the CCA-SJ;
- promote meetings to present results;
- record development activities in the military's curriculum; and
- issue certificates for performed jobs.

As to the low level of satisfaction in the relationship with superiors, the following objective was defined:

- to hold weekly meetings with staff, addressing issues related to work environment.

The following objectives were established to solve internal communication problems:

- to perform group dynamics about communication; and
- to establish processes for information flow between Teams and Sections.

Finally, regarding the lack of support from the chain of command, the PMO itself was in charge of identifying the needs of Teams and taking necessary actions.

2.4   Problem Solving

Monitoring meetings were estabilished so that Product Owners can update projects statuses.

During the first monitoring meeting, problems with other projects were identified. It was also identified that the statuses of some projects were not presented by Product Owners, but by the highest ranked military within the Development Team.

The first two meetings were made with a month apart. Guidelines were issued to standardizing processes, correcting problems, among others. It was identified lacks of communication between Development Teams and upper echelons.

Prior to the third monitoring meeting, it was decided to make weekly meetings following Scrum Daily Meetings format. PMO and Product Owners were the participants. After that, Product Owners were well oriented and prepared to present status of projects and also to address problems.

After that, communication channels were opened and informations flowed. Problems started to be identified in advance, minimizing impacts due to delays in solutions.

Thus, the PMO also decided to use Scrum to follow up projects and systems under development in the CCA-SJ. By this way, another object was set: to run weekly meetings with Product Owners and Scrum Masters.

Meetings with Product Owners are already performed. As for Scrum Masters, they were invited to the following monitoring meetings. Weekly meetings will also be done with Scrum Masters.

2.5   Trainings

The need for training was identified from the beginning, since Scrum was adopted in the CCA-SJ only based on previous knowledge of some.

A partnership with ITA allows some CCA-SJ military to participate in a dynamic for basic understandings of Scrum. The dynamic "Lego4Scrum" is delivered at the beginning of each semester to undergraduate and graduate students of ITA's Computer Engineering. Eventually, according to the availability of vacancies, CCA-SJ's military are invited to participate, In the first half of 2018, 18 (eighteen) have participated in the training.

However, this training is not enough, since it is only 3 hours long. In this way, the PMO identified the need for other trainings, prioritizing the following: Agile Coach, for 3 PMO members, and Professional Scrum Product Owner (PSPO), aimed to 10 (ten) Product Owners of Development Teams.

It is expected that the Scrum and its good practices will be internalized in the CCA-SJ.

3   Results

Although this is a work in progress, after the beginning of the Action Plan, several improvements were identified in processes and even in the quality of delivered products.

Once Development Teams started to make technical decisions, they have afforded immediate results in software quality, better prioritization of User Stories, and better assistance to the chain of command.

A fraternization event was held at the end of june, with a lunch to all staff, marking the end of first semester. In the event, several results were presented, perspectives for the next semester, certificates were delivered to Development Teams, among others. The result of the event was very positive and, together with other actions being taken, the military feel more motivated and worth in their work environment nowadays. It is still early to raise performance indicators, but the expectation is for improved productivity.

With frequent meetings and the above mentioned fraternization event, superiors are being encouraged to interact better with their subordinates.

Communication problems were minimized. Monitoring meetings and Weekly Meetings with Product Owners allowed the chain of command better projects monitoring. In addition, processes of communication between sections have been improved.

The view of lack of support from the chain of command has been modified. The truth is that there was a lack of transparency in some actions. Topics were taken to weekly meetings. From then on, staff became more motivated to work. The expected result is increased productivity.

4   Final Considerations

At the beginning of PMO works, based on the satisfaction survey conducted with Development Teams, some factors were identified that had a negative influence on the level of satisfaction of some military in their work environment, which reflected the productivity of these military personnel and the quality of products.

These factors led PMO to draw up an Action Plan to allow the use of Scrum within this strongly hierarchical environment.

Although it is work in progress, the performance of the PMO in the CCA-SJ managed to minimize several of the problems identified.

Some results were obtained in a shorter period, mainly the improvement in communication and motivation.

With the training planned for the second semester, it is expected the improvement in the processes and the consequent increase in the quality of developed products.

The next step is to provide trainings for Scrum Masters and Development Teams, held by PMO. These trainings are planned to the end of october.

References

1. BRASIL: Constituição da República Federativa do Brasil de (1988)
2. BRASIL: Estatuto dos Militares. Lei 6.880 de 9 de dezembro de 1980 (1980)
3. BRASIL: ROCA 21–9/2011 Regulamento de Centro de Computação da Aeronáutica (2011)
4. Cohn, M.: Desenvolvimento de Software com Scrum: aplicando métodos ágeis com sucesso. Grupo A Bookman (2000)
5. Schwaber, K., Sutherland, J.: Um guia definitivo para o Scrum: As regras do jogo (2013). https://www.scrumguides.org/docs/scrumguide/v1/Scrum-Guide-Portuguese-BR.pdf

Author Index

Borges, Marcos A. F.   63

Cesa, Luiz Otávio Aléssio   19
Corrêa Rodrigues, Adriana   49
Cursino, Rodrigo   3

de Matos, Altieres   34
de Oliveira, Adelmo Dias   97
de Resende Lucas, Everton Luiz   97
de Sá, Fernando Rodrigues   97
de Souza Gimenes, Itana Maria   80

Farias, João   3

Graciotto Silva, Marco Aurélio   34

Lancastre, Maria   3

Malucelli, Andreia   19
Mantovani Fontana, Rafaela   19, 49

Ré, Reginaldo   34
Reinehr, Sheila   19
Ribeiro, Marcelo Lessa   80

Sambinelli, Fernando   63
Santos, Wylliams   3

Printed in the United States
By Bookmasters

Printed in the United States
By Bookmasters